BUB

Essays from Just North of Nashville

DREW BRATCHER

UNIVERSITY OF IOWA PRESS

Iowa City

University of Iowa Press, Iowa City 52242
Copyright © 2022 by Drew Bratcher
uipress.uiowa.edu
Printed in the United States of America
ISBN 978-1-60938-849-2 (pbk)
ISBN 978-1-60938-850-2 (ebk)

Text design by Richard Hendel

Printed on acid-free paper

Cataloging-in-Publication data is on file with the
Library of Congress.

BUB

for Emily

CONTENTS

If only one knew what to remember or pretend to remember.

— ELIZABETH HARDWICK,
   Sleepless Nights

BUB

You asked me once what I thought I would remember most about him, and I said, straightaway, his ear.

His ear? you asked.

His ear, I repeated, more confidently this time, though in truth the answer surprised me too. While it seemed to have sprung from some deep, unfiltered place, I could not recall ever paying his ear—or any ear for that matter—much regard.

I might have answered any number of ways. Might have said his hands, for instance. The hulking grace of his hands around a knife or a spit cup or a cane handle. I might have said his voice, which for the longest time I listened to and tried to follow whenever I told a story. I might have said something about the bracing force of his presence in the world, which was a kind of omnipresence, something I would look back on later as an early intimation of God.

I might have said it was impossible to choose one thing.

Yet in that moment a retrieval happened. I sensed my mind or something behind my mind racing as if to recover lost ground. The idea became a shadow, became the thing that threw the shadow, until I held suspended in thought, of all things, the image of my grandfather's ear.

He was driving. I was in the seat behind him. I was asking about a road sign I'd seen through the front window. Black letters on a yellow diamond said Falling Rock. I'd never seen a sign like that, and I'd seen my share of signs. Dead End. One Way. Low Clearing. School Zone. Speed Limit 25. Speed Limit 65. Railroad Crossing. Tractor Crossing. Pedestrian Crossing. Deer Crossing. And, at the bend in the road between my grandparents' house and ours, Wild Turkey Crossing Use Caution Please.

In an effort to escape the carsickness that swept over me whenever my eyes veered too far from the front window, I had, by necessity, become something of a sentinel. And not only for road signs but also for out-of-state plates, billboards, storm clouds, roadkill, abandoned vehicles, roadside memorials, vultures, historical markers, deer in the offing, airplanes, church steeples, you name it. But Falling Rock? As in, heads up? Incoming? Fore!? This was new, striking, and it must be said, however silly it seems to me now, cause for alarm.

A few months earlier, my uncle had been in a wreck between Nashville and Chattanooga. His face was a blue-and-red marble. His car was a wad of twisted metal. Whispers in the house hinted at bad trouble, but no one would tell me what happened.

It had been night out, that much I knew. I knew my uncle, who watched NASCAR for the crashes, had not been driving slow. Now I wondered whether a boulder, hurtling downhill at a high speed, could have been what knocked him off the road.

What I needed to know was whether the sign's strange pronouncement should be taken seriously, whether the showers of stone it conjured posed a real and urgent threat. And so, to the sound of my voice, no doubt weakened by fear and ignorance, and made more tremulous than usual by the rutted Tennessee two-lane, my grandfather had inclined his big right ear.

It was big, yes, but not so out of sync with the rest of him. Work had warped my grandfather's body, aging, distending everything. He was oversized but oversized all over. His sags and bulges, considerable in places, maintained a kind of structural integrity by dint of his personal style and grooming routine.

He trimmed his mustache every morning. He combed and combed a head of smoke-white hair. He belted his slacks up over his stomach, kept his button-downs pressed, his shirttails buried. Except before bed, when he removed his false teeth and his whole face imploded, he was proportionate to himself in total, distinguished, handsome even, in his heavy way.

Isolated, though, his ear was an enormity of flesh and cartilage. The swoop of the scapha, the jut and droop of the lobe, they gave it nothing if not the air of a question mark. Among the many inquiries it might have punctuated—such as who was this man, and what did I mean him?—was a glaring one about the ear itself.

Along the top curve, a portion of the flap was missing. It looked as if it had been pinned back, sheared away. Had he been born that way? Had he been in a fight? Had something got hold of his ear? I didn't have the nerve to ask.

Then one morning, as we were feeding the beagle pups in the pen behind his house, he told me the story. He had tripped over the water hose and, in a wild flail to keep from crashing, had slashed his knuckle on the rusty chain-link fence. On the walk back to the house, he listed along the fencerow, halted not mainly by the fall, though his hand must have been burning, but by far-off thoughts that had been reassembled, all of a sudden, by the confluence of blood, dog, and flesh.

The story went that one morning when he was young, his old man—a coal miner who moonlit as a barber in the West Virginia holler where they lived—ordered his five boys to the front porch for haircuts. My grandfather was the oldest. He was first up in the chair. "Sit your ass still," my great-grandfather told him, then added, "if you want to keep your goddamn ear."

In later years, my great-grandfather would become something of a sweetheart. He played the banjo. He told corny jokes in quiet, high-pitched tones. He slipped me candy when my mother wasn't looking. But even at his warmest, his goofiest, he was remote. His name was Enos after an obscure figure from the book of Genesis. His ring finger on his right hand had been mangled in a mining accident. Rather than have the finger taken off, he'd let it heal on its own. It had reset at a ninety-degree angle. When you shook his hand, the finger pressed against your palm, keeping you at bay. Sometimes, I think of that finger in the ground where he is buried, standoffish as ever, and unmistakable, among the decaying bones.

Enos's specialty was the bowl cut. On the porch that day, he placed a mixing bowl on my grandfather's head. He cut around the rim with scissors he sharped on a grindstone. Hair fell onto my grandfather's shoulders, fell onto the chairback, onto the worn porch boards. It drifted onto his nose as well. Tingled like crazy. Set his nostrils on fire.

Within seconds of his reaching up to scratch the itch, my great-grandfather had made good on the warning. He snicked a flap off the top of my grandfather's ear, then went right on cutting through the gore. Before my grandfather could register the cut, before he thought about going for the part of his ear that had gone missing, then thought again for fear that further movement might prompt his father to lop off the rest, the dog had leapt onto the porch.

She lapped at the blood. She took the little piece of flesh between her teeth and went to town.

All that was there, I told you, when my grandfather turned his head. And there I was, too. Five or six years old. Red in the cheeks. Forever on the cusp of motion sickness. Not beyond picking my nose and eating it when no one was looking. Not beyond being scared stupid by a highway sign.

Held shell-like to my own, I imagine my grandfather's ear humming with geography and weather and something like the century itself, with wild animals, howling wind, and country music, with the words of his mother and uncles and his own grandparents, people who had long since vanished but whose voices went on sounding, if nowhere else in the universe, deep down in my grandfather's ear. Now, by some fluke of proximity, it was open to me.

What had I said to get his attention? What was he thinking about when I called out his name? Had I said anything about the sign? Anything about my uncle? Certainly nothing about my worries, for which I could hardly have had a language. Certainly nothing about my fears.

It was a minor gesture, just a centimeter's tilt of the head, really, not enough to pull his eyes from the road. Nothing he had not done a thousand times before. Except that this time I registered it even as I awaited his reply.

And how had he answered? An Indian princess, he said, had gone missing in those parts. Her mother and father had been searching night and day. She was tough as limestone. She was quick as rivers. Her name, of course, was Falling Rock. Keep a look out, my grandfather told me, whoever finds her is sure to come into a reward.

Needless to say, I looked.

For miles and miles, I kept the watch, hazarding the nausea and dizziness all the while, redirected from the dread stirred by that yellow placard into a landscape where search parties combed the piney woods and finding what was missing was no more impracticable than spotting a motorcycle with California tags or a mountain lion heeled up beside a telephone pole.

I never found Falling Rock. She was not something you could find, yet I sensed, for a while at least, until sleep stole into the backseat like a veiled desperado, that I had come into a reward all the same.

Then again, I might have said his hands. They were like stones pulled from a creek bed, their heavy roughness had been burnished to a smooth regard. They were pockmarked. They were enormous. On one finger he wore a wedding ring, on another a Masonic ring. Around his wrist there was a gold watch and a copper bracelet. Needless to say, he had a firm grip.

In the casket, his hands were folded over the buttons of his blue pinstripe jacket, empty but for each other, as they'd rarely been in life. I wanted to reach in and unclasp them. I wanted to sink his hands into his back pockets the way he'd stand in the yard in the mornings, surveying the fruit trees and pasture in the fog.

I thought of kings and queens buried holding scepters and rods and the symbols of power, of Frank Sinatra and his bottle of Jack, the Mahler score placed over Leonard Bernstein's heart. For my grandfather, the contents of his pockets would have sufficed: that southern trinity of tobacco, pocketknife, and comb.

He chewed Beech-Nut. He went through a bag every three, four days. He'd done so for as long as I could remember. I had seen old photos of him smoking cigars. There was a pipe stand above the liquor cabinet in his office downtown. Dottle filled your mouth when you sucked at the stems. But it was Beech-Nut that kept him in business, or was it the other way around? When he died, my brother and I joked about some young exec in corporate trying to account for the sudden plummet in sales.

With its pattern of fanned-out, red-and-white stripes, the foldable Beech-Nut bag was like a flag declaring what? His dependency, I reckon. But also his history. Beech-Nut was what Enos chewed. Cigarettes, they were lightning in the mine. Sparks ignited firedamp, pent-up pockets of carbon dioxide and methane gas. So Enos chewed and spit more or less all day, and as he spit he shoveled coal from a thirty-inch seam. On his knees. This was in Mingo County, ten miles up the Tug Fork River from Matewan, where the Coal Wars had commenced a couple of decades earlier.

Postshift, he trudged across the mountain path to his shack in Turkey Creek, where in the center of the main room, my great-grandmother filled a No. 3 washtub half full of stove-boiled well water. She washed Enos's back and helped him wash (*warsh* in her pronunciation) his hair. When he got through bathing, the water was ink.

There's a song by Roy Clark, later covered by Johnny Cash, called "I Never Picked Cotton." The song's narrator is a loose cannon with a caustic wit. He's left the family farm in Okla-

homa to pursue a life of carousing and petty theft. After skirt-
ing the law for years, he's finally been apprehended for killing
a redneck in Memphis. As he awaits the gallows, he thinks
back over his life. His greatest accomplishment, he concludes,
isn't anything he's achieved. What he's most proud of is what
he hasn't done. "But I never picked cotton," the chorus goes,
"Like my mother did and my brother did / And my sister did
and my daddy died young / Workin' in the coal mine."

Like the man in the song, my grandfather bucked family
tradition. For certain he was proud he never dug coal. It was
an act of resistance that came naturally enough, which is
not to say easily, and yet his respect for his father's labors,
which must have accounted in part for his father's severity,
prevented him from saying so. Had he ever been inside the
mine for himself? He and his buddies, he told me, would
sometimes commandeer empty coal carts when the mine was
closed, touching a metal pole to the rail to get a jolt. The truth
is, he talked about coal rarely, if at all. Even so, he referenced
the mines indirectly—and must occasionally have thought of
Enos, hunkered over, digging by the light of a carbide head-
lamp—when he took the tobacco pouch from his pocket and
extracted a wad.

Unlike snuff, a pinch of which you placed behind your bottom lip and which supplied a quick and surprisingly potent
buzz, chaw was a slower, sloppier ordeal. It was also tougher
to conceal. One day in middle school, I left my folder under
my desk in geography class. Stepping back into the classroom,
I was surprised to see the teacher, an old man whose dress-
shirt sleeves were forever rolled above his considerable forearms, spitting into his Coke can as he erased the chalkboard.
It turned out the whole time he'd been up there talking about
the weather and topographical features of countries on the
other side of the world, he'd had a dip in!

Such antics were impossible with chew tobacco. It filled

your lower jaw and the pout above your chin and generated an unconscionable amount of saliva, which had to be hocked, especially early on in the chew, almost constantly. Even if you could hide the wad behind, say, a thick beard or, as in my grandfather's case, a heavy jowl, speech would give you away. Talking while chewing tobacco is like walking with a full cup of coffee. Do so too fast and you risk a spill.

My grandfather wasn't trying to hide anything. He chewed with such comfort and consistency that any initial shock or revulsion you felt soon faded. The spits he made into his Styrofoam cup, which he padded with paper towels to absorb the saliva and limit backsplash, were like reverse sips from the same. His slow, occasionally slobbering way of speaking became his speech. Over the course of the telling, his stories certified themselves. But in retrospect, it's clear that their pacing was as much a function of his habit than a pure response to the demands of narrative.

Smoking created a different effect. When my uncle talked, the cigarette in his hand delineated his gesticulations. The flick of the ash marked time. Smoke was like a baton with which he conducted speech, a prop that enhanced the performance. But my grandfather's Beech-Nut was part of the script. It imbued his pronouncements with a watery undertow, a muted strain that gave gravity—and a touch of suspense—to his words.

At one time or another, the grandkids all tried it, sneaking a pouch of Beech-Nut from the console in the El Camino or from the table beside his armchair, not because he wouldn't have given us a plug if we'd asked him for it, but because we wanted to be ready when that moment came. Retreating to the barn loft or crouching behind a hay bale on his front pasture, we were surprised by the texture of the tobacco, like the fringed leather on a cowboy shirt, by the tough and tender juiciness of it, by the slow and noxious burn, and then the flood.

We spit and spit but discovered only more saliva each time until we spit out the chaw altogether and found, to our surprise, that the saliva kept flowing—an hour later, you were still spitting, still picking tobacco out of your teeth—and we wondered how he made it look so natural, so simple to control, like a cow chewing cud, when we were cats hocking hairballs.

One plug could last him the better part of the day. When he was done chewing, he'd take the spent wad into his hand, walk over to the fencerow, and flat-hand it to one of the horses, who he swore loved the stuff, a contention that was impossible to prove but that the horses' satisfied chomps seemed to concede.

Mouth cancer, that's what chewing tobacco was supposed to give you, or at the very least bad trouble with your gums and teeth, but his dental hygiene had bottomed out years before I was born. Now, he had perfect teeth, which is to say false ones.

It was a shock when he removed the pair. In those moments, he turned twenty years older, rougher. He could have been one of the hobos ambling down the railroad track behind my uncle's house and that my mother told us to pray for but to be wary of. He could have been the older brother of Pockets, the bum in overalls who sat on the pew outside Food Town grocery, stammering nonsense while sucking on a Yoo-hoo through a straw.

My grandfather's teeth had rotted out around the time he moved to Nashville. Dr. Bryant, the local dentist, suggested dentures. My grandfather, who was trying to get a new business off the ground, couldn't afford them. The doctor said it was urgent. My grandfather said he couldn't pay him in cash, but he could pay him with a pony. They made a deal, choppers for a horse, a trade that endeared him to the dentist, who was also my dentist and who told me the story whenever he checked my teeth for cavities.

Each night, my grandfather soaked his dentures in solution. Garbled and askew while he rinsed them in the morning, his voice became clearer, louder, like some far-off radio station coming into range, as he gummed his teeth back into place. Before he ate a fried egg or finished his first cup of coffee, before he fed the dogs, watered the horses, or washed his hair, he put in a wad of tobacco and chewed.

In his pants' pockets, he also kept a pocketknife, pearl-handled, with a locking clip-point blade. He trimmed his fingernails with it, cutting V's into the middles to keep the nails, he swore, from growing into the quicks.

His hands were steady like his mother's. She threaded needles, shucked corn, and snapped beans with indefatigable precision. Her name was Elmay (pronounced Elmy). I called her Mammaw Ray. She hoed hard rows in rocky mountain soil. Pickled everything. Kept beehives too, reaching in without gloves to extract the comb.

Once she threw a carving knife at Enos when he came home drunk and tried to lay hands on her. The blade missed him but missed by just enough to convince him that she could have hit him if she'd had a mind to. I can't remember who first told me this story, but I cannot recall a time when I didn't know it, and I remember thinking, as I sat beside my great-grandmother in a rocking chair while she snapped beans and hummed hymns about Heaven, that the same hands that washed Enos clean could have killed Enos dead, and I remember feeling awe in her presence, that heady mix of pride and praise and fear.

There's a song by Holly Dunn called "Daddy's Hands," in which the singer catalogs her father's life through his fingers and palms. "Daddy's hands," she sings, "were soft and kind when I was cryin' / Daddy's hands were hard as steel when I'd done wrong." They held hammers; they comforted her mama. Tough or tender, Dunn concludes, in the song's penultimate line, "There was always love in daddy's hands." In Bill Withers's "Grandma's Hands," kindness ("Grandma's hands soothed a local unwed mother") and caution ("Grandma's hands used to issue out a warning / She'd say, 'Billy don't you run so fast') characterize the old woman's touch.

Whatever else you could say about my grandfather's hands,

what they had in spades was exactitude. They were like worn tools of which he was in total command. He buried nails in boards with two clean blows. Whirled rope into unbreakable knots. Tied floss to the back legs of June bugs, no problem, and let me fly the green critters around the yard. The cars he detailed came out looking brand new.

His gift proved to be a burden as other parts of his body broke down and he was forced to tap other people for jobs he could do quicker and with more precision. Five years before I was born, a tractor jumped gears while he was under it and ran over him, breaking his back in three places. Surgeries ensued. He lost a couple of inches. His spine never healed right. From then on he was reliant on others for the heavy lifting. He would stand with his hands in his back pockets, watching instead of working, biting his tongue, which was its own kind of work for him.

He hired me once to paint the boards around the ceiling of his porch. As he looked on, his hands in his back pockets, I climbed the wooden stepstool. I dipped the brush in the paint bucket and proceeded to cover the board. But I'd put too much paint on the brush and applied too much pressure to the wood. White paint streamed down the board and splattered beneath me. Agitated, beet-faced, he swiped the brush from my shaking hand. In four or five clean strokes, he corrected my mistake, covering the board in question, then moving on to the others. Afterward, he tried to show me how to do it. But it was of no use. I didn't have his hands.

With his pocketknife, my grandfather peeled turnips, peeled potatoes, peeled and sliced all kinds of fruit. He had a vegetable garden round the side of his house, an orchard out back. There were three or four varieties of apples, some red, some green. There were pears, plums, white peaches. For a week, maybe two, until the birds and squirrels caught the scent, cherries ripened on a little tree leaning over the barnyard fence. There was even a vine of concord grapes, which my grandmother made into jelly.

One Friday night, when I was sixteen years old, I drove up to see my grandfather. An hour earlier, in the parking lot of Grace Baptist Church around the bend from my high school, I had confessed my love to a girl whose boyfriend had gone off to college but who had been spending a lot of time driving around with me after school. A lifetime of bad country lyrics sprang from my tongue. I told her I loved her, that I couldn't live without her. But as in so many country songs, I had gotten the wrong impression. It turned out she was going to marry the college boy (as indeed she did). Riding away I felt some combination of guilty, silly, sad, and confused.

I found my grandfather sitting on his back porch. He was wearing nothing but his underwear and a white V-neck T-shirt. The fan wobbled overhead. Moths slapped at the yellow porchlight. With his pocketknife, he was peeling apples.

"I was just thinking about you," he said, as I came through the screen door. "Take a seat," he said. "Tell me what's on your mind."

I tried to explain about the girl. As he peeled, halved, cored, and quartered apples, he listened to me. When I was finished, he said, "Hand me another one of them apples, would you now. Your grandmother's making a pie."

I handed him an apple. He took it in his right hand. With his left, he slipped the knife beneath the surface and pulled it toward him, using his thumb to rotate the fruit. Slowly the rind began to release its hold. He turned and turned the fruit beneath his thumb, the knife pulling all the while in the opposite direction, and still the skin did not break. It dangled from the fruit, then dropped onto the table in a single unbroken ribbon. He picked it up and handed it to me. I looked at him, half wondering whether he wanted me to take a bite.

"Throw that over your shoulder," he said.

I looked at him, not understanding.

"Over your shoulder," he said, and made the motion.

"Toward the screen?" I said.

"Just throw the damn thing over your shoulder," he said again.

I wadded the peel into a ball and tossed it behind me. It hit the porch screen, scattering moths, and landed on the floor.

"Now," he said. "What letter did it make when it landed?"

"Letter?" I said.

"The old timers used to say," he said, "if you threw an apple peel over your shoulder like that, the letter it made would be the first letter of your true love's name."

I stood up and turned around to get a better look.

"What letter do you see?" he said.

"I can't tell," I said.

"Look closer," he said. "What letter?"

I bent down to where the peel had fallen in a kind of ring intersected by the tail end. "I don't know," I said. "Maybe a Q."

"Q, huh?" he said.

"That's right," I said. "And I can't think of a single name that starts with a Q, can you?"

He laughed. "Son," he said, "that's the best one. That means she's going to be a Queen."

Next to the tobacco pouch in my grandfather's back pocket was a hair comb. It was black, plastic. Nothing fancy. He had three or four he'd cycle through. In his bathroom after the funeral, they were lined up on the counter as if awaiting new orders.

His hair was white, wavy. He never did go bald. Starting at the crown, then moving across his scalp in three or four oscillating strokes, he'd bend his loose waves to a composed billow before finishing with a couple of flicks above his right and left ear. There was something boyish in the motion. With the comb in his hand, he was a snotnose standing before a mirror, a teenybopper getting ready for a date. There was also something assertive. He was a young buck headed into a job interview, a grown man getting ready to walk his daughter down the aisle. There was a way to tell the story of his life through the comb, the black tines moving through hair slowly changing color.

He was blonde when he met my grandmother. They were classmates at Belfry High, in Pike County, Kentucky, a mile from the West Virginia border. Her father, Homer, was also a coal miner. Although they had been in school together all along, he had not noticed her until junior year when, in—*What class was it again, Barbara? Science, I guess. Ah, yes, biology*—he heard laughter, looked across the room, and saw a pretty girl in the back row with an aquiline nose and a head full of green hair.

Her name was Barbara. The night before, giving in to the urges of her younger sister, Judy, she'd attempted to dye her dark brown hair blonde with a box solution and ended up with a patch of grass instead. She was mortified, but her mother, Bertha, wouldn't hear about her skipping.

I said to myself, my grandfather would say, recalling the first time he saw her, "Who in the world is this?"

It was a Friday morning. There was a football game that night. After class, he walked over and asked her to go with him. When she said yes, he told her he'd pick her up; then he remembered he didn't have a car. His red '48 Frazer was out of commission. His uncle Pry, however, had a Pontiac available. There was only one problem, it was wrecked. The passenger side door had been smashed in a collision with a coal truck. It was still parked in the yard, waiting to be inspected by an insurance adjustor. He talked Pry into letting him take the Pontiac. When he picked my grandmother up before the game, she had to get in on his side. He was worried she'd be embarrassed by the car. She was afraid he'd be embarrassed by her hair. Chagrin endeared them. Each was too embarrassed to be embarrassed of the other. By the time they went on a second date, her hair was brown again, and he'd got his Frazer up and running. Not long after that, he traded it for a

'51 Chevy, using the money he'd made working at a service station on the weekend and at the drive-in theater on weeknights to put a new engine in it and make it shine.

How many steering wheels passed through my grandfather's fingers? A child of his generation, he was obsessed with cars. And yet cars also seemed to match his disposition. He was smooth yet propulsive. He got things moving without ever seeming to be in a hurry. He was at rest going high speeds over rough terrain. Insofar as he had one, his seat of power was the seat of a car.

He remembered going with his father across the mountain to trade a horse for an old Model T, which Enos learned how to drive on the way home. Roads were ruddy, sometimes nonexistent. Even in the 1990s, when we'd drive up from Tennessee to see my great-grandparents, you had to get off the highway and take back roads for fifty or sixty miles to reach their holler, going up and around one mountain and up and around the next on two-lane roads with very little in the way of a shoulder, and when you looked out the window, you could see, especially in the winter, the skeletons of cars that had gone over the edge. At one point on the way back, Enos tried to cross a creek but didn't give the Model T enough gas to get over the bank on the other side. The car, famously top heavy, toddled onto its side. How they got it back upright, I don't know. They had to push it the rest of the way home.

Cars, they could take you places. Even before my grandfather could drive, town exerted a heavy pull. Buoyed by veterans returning from the war and by a bump in the demand for coal power, Williamson was bustling in the 1950s. There was a Sears Roebuck, a pharmacy, a bank, a hotel, restaurants, a salon. My grandfather kept a plywood boat on the bank of the Tug River and rowed over whenever he could. Later, he would drive into town with my grandmother's father, Homer, who knew what doors to knock on to procure a jug of whiskey.

All I know about Homer is that he liked to drink and fight. The bars in Williamson were on a street called Deep Third.

One day, my grandfather and Homer were walking back to their car. At a cross street, Homer pushed him against the side of a building.

"When I say the word," he said. "I want you to take off running."

"How come?" my grandfather asked.

Homer said a roughneck was following them but not to worry, he knew what to do. My grandfather was supposed to take off running up the street. Meanwhile, Homer would hide against the wall. When the man ran by, he'd clock him.

They waited a few moments. When Homer gave the command, my grandfather took off.

Sure enough, the man followed. A moment later, my grandfather heard a pop. When he turned around, he saw the man on the ground, Homer standing over him.

"What now?" my grandfather hollered.

Already moving, Homer answered, "Now we both run."

Another thing I know about Homer: When my grandparents got pregnant with their first, he had so resolved in his mind that the grandbaby was going to be a boy (he had had three daughters) that when my mother was born he took to calling her Deborah John.

My grandfather combs his hair again and he's out of school. He's on a railroad track outside Williamson in the winter. He makes fifty dollars for an eight-hour shift. The key on his belt fits the lock on the metal switch, but when he turns it, the lock doesn't budge. The train he's on needs to get into a spur so that another train can pass by. There's no time, though. He can hear the other train approaching. His captain sees what's happening and yells for the crew to bail.

The train hits them going forty miles per hour. It smashes the back railcar and knocks three or four others off the track. No one dies, but the damage is substantial. In the ensuing trial, the union lawyer counsels him to emphasize how new he is to the job, less than a year. He's to say he's still learning the ropes.

He's exonerated, but shortly thereafter, his conductor, whose hair Enos cuts on the porch every two weeks, pulls him aside. He tells him there's no future in railroading. He says he's been working on trains for thirty years and still can't secure a day shift. Railroad companies had already begun replacing manual switches with electric ones that don't need key switches. The conductor tells him his days are numbered, that if he knows what's good for him he'll get out.

He combs his hair, which by his midtwenties is already turning silver around his temples, and he's in a car, riding roads around Pikeville, Kentucky, where he and my grandmother, married now and with a baby on the way, have moved for work. He's doing repo for a regional bank with national aspirations. He pays visits to customers who've fallen behind. They write him a check or he takes their vehicle. Hard driving, he puts a hundred thousand plus miles on the odometer a year. One trip, he blows out a brand-new set of Atlas tires in two days.

You've got to be young. You've got to be fearless. You sure as hell can't overthink it. You've got to be impulsive—*ignorant*, he told me once—to do this kind of work.

There's one customer he's been looking for, for seven months. He has a two-tone Ford in white and blue. He hasn't made a single payment since he signed the lease. Whenever he drives by the man's house, he looks for the car, never sees it. Sometimes he goes so far as to pull into the driveway. He walks to the door and knocks, cups his hands against the window. Once, the wife answers. "Out of town," she says. "No, I don't know when he's coming back."

Then one day, on a drive back to Pikeville from Prestonsburg, he looks down the driveway as he passes the house and sees the damn thing. It's sitting out front, facing the road.

In the shotgun seat beside him sits Earl Lever, a war vet with a young family who will do just about anything for extra cash. He's hard working and loyal, sometimes loyal to a fault. Once, Earl was behind the wheel of a repo that wouldn't run. They'd attached it to my grandfather's car with a six-foot chain. A few miles down the dirt road stood a hitchhiker, and when Earl, who had forgotten he was being towed, hit the brakes to offer him a ride, the bumper came right off the car.

My grandfather pulls into the driveway and parks beside the Ford. He tells Earl to get behind the wheel. He tells him to stay ready. They may have to make a run for it. He gets out of the car, looks through the window of the Ford. The keys are in the ignition. This time, when he knocks on the door of the house, a man answers. He has a bottle in his hand. He sways in the doorjamb, slurring his words.

My grandfather tells him what he's come to do.

"No, sir," the man says. "I can't let you have my car."

My grandfather says he can keep the car if he can make a payment. The man says he doesn't have money but can borrow some.

"Come with me," my grandfather says.

He holds open the back door of his car and the man ducks into the backseat. My grandfather gets in beside him.

"Tell Earl here where you want us to go," he says.

First up, the grocery store. The man walks in and walks out empty-handed. They go to the hardware store next, then the feedlot. "I reckon I'm not going to be able to give you any money today," the man says.

Back at the house, he tells them he has a few more people to call on. He tells them to come back tomorrow morning. He'll have their money. "OK," my grandfather says. "We'll see you tomorrow."

But after the man goes inside, my grandfather makes for the Ford. He opens the door, turns the key. The car doesn't want to run. He turns the key again, revs the engine. He's only just got it going when he hears the first blast. He looks in the rearview mirror. The man is standing on the porch with a 12-gauge rifle aimed at the car.

My grandfather motions for Earl to drive, and he takes off behind him, kicking up dust and gravel. He hears more pops as he speeds down the driveway. Then he hears glass shatter and feels shards stabbing into his neck and shoulders. When he looks down, his white shirt is covered in blood.

He skids onto the main road and speeds away. Finally out of rifle range, he passes Earl and steers for the police department in town to file a report. Inside, the sheriff ushers my grandfather into his office. He gives him a rag and a bottle of rubbing alcohol to dab at his neck.

"Who did that to you? . . . Oh, him."

The man had recently been released from an asylum in Lexington.

"It took five of us to get him in the car to take him there," the sheriff says. "Good thing he was drunk. Otherwise, I doubt you'd have made it out of there with your life."

The bank moves him all over. He combs his blonde hair in Boone, North Carolina; his silver hair in Charleston, South Carolina; his white hair in east and then middle Tennessee. He has two children, two years between them. My mother, who has his dimples. My uncle, who has his Ball jar–blue eyes.

He leaves the bank. Opens his own outfit in Nashville, leasing vehicles and heavy equipment across the midstate. Starts building houses on the side, tries his luck with an oil well, self-publishes a cookbook called *Grandmother's Cupboard* with a dedication that reads "Dedicated to all our mothers and grandmothers, who worked so hard to feed us so well with so little." He weighs three hundred pounds.

He goes to a doctor for something or other, and the doctor refuses treatment.

"How come?" he says.

"Because your head's about to blow off," the doctor says.

Instead of pork rinds and gas station specials, he eats five pounds a day of carrots, celery, cabbage. He's a rabbit driving up and down the highway signing leases. He's a long way from home, but, he jokes, he's finally a coal miner, all that slack in his pants.

Of the many cars my grandfather drove, the one he loved most was a white El Camino. From Enos's Model T to the Jaguars and Mercedes he bought and sold, to the antique Bugatti he entered in the Fourth of July parade several summers in a row, the El Camino is the one that will still be in his driveway the day he dies. It's his Elijah's chariot, the one car he would have picked, if such a choice had been presented, to ride away in.

It's a 1986 model, released a year before Chevrolet ceased production. Call it Chevy's take on the minotaur. Half hot rod, half pickup, entirely shameless. With its sharp edges and silver runners, combed back into a slick mullet of truck bed, the El Camino, Spanish for the "The Way," seems engineered to be all things to all rednecks, as fit for drag racing on Friday night as hauling hay the Saturday morning after.

My grandfather does neither. To him the El Camino is some kind of symbol, perhaps even a totem. The in-betweenness seems emblematic, the way the vehicle is not fully the one thing or fully the other, the way it's both and neither and somehow nowhere anymore. The way it leans in both directions: toward eccentricity, away from opulence. How it's parked halfway between past and present. How there's no back seat in it either, nowhere to hide.

I could hardly see over the dashboard when my grandfather first took me riding in the El Camino. One hand on the wheel, the other gripping a spit cup, he steered the overgrown back country north of Nashville. The roads were slim and sidewinding. Concrete gave way to gravel and dirt the farther we strayed.

From the fingers lifted on passing steering wheels and the hats tipped from roadside plots, it was clear the El Camino was some kind of celebrity in those parts, the cockier cousin of the half-buried Monte Carlos and Rancheros in the hillside junkyards blurring by.

Weak-stomached from motion sickness, I strained to keep my eyes on the yellow lines, but the country's odd frames taunted me through the El Camino's long windows. Barns falling in on themselves like toothless faces. Gourd trees and yard ornaments. Jackasses twitching behind splintered fences. It took but a glance in the direction of my grandfather's nod for a wave of nausea to sweep over me and turn the joyride into rolling torture.

I despaired at the thought of failing him, at flashing weakness where there ought to have been a callus of steel, so I palmed the leather seats as if the El Camino were a bull to ride. The truth is, I dreaded the El Camino more than school or the doctor's office. Following each ride, I vowed to sit out the next one, but when the invitation repeated, my grandfather calling out my name through the wafting exhaust, a yen for his company and a doggedness to prove myself worthy of it shoveled over the discomfort the road ahead was already rearing to resurrect.

When the time came for me to learn how to drive, the two of us swapped places. The carsickness no longer an issue from the driver's side, I circled the pasture and finagled the orchard on the slope behind my grandfather's house. I had mowed and bushhogged this land since elementary school, swiping low fruit, sometimes even steering with my knees, but in the car the confident recklessness with which I maneuvered the tractor gave way to vigilance. I was a benchwarmer given an at bat in a big inning, my one goal in the world not to make a fool of myself.

On the concrete driveway, which veered down the hillside for a quarter mile and held the front pasture in a loose headlock, the El Camino picked up speed without my touching the gas. We blew past the horses on the front pasture. The toms on the lip of the woods wobbled into the roughage. What must have been twenty miles per hour seemed like Mach 2; for a moment, my mind went white and my boots lost touch of the pedal.

I found and punched the brake. The El Camino slammed to a stop, then pitched forward. The tires squealed like beagle pups snagged on barbed wire. In the silence that followed, I waited for a censure, for the cold blue of my grandfather's eyes to cut across my mug. But if he was perturbed, he gave no indication.

"Give it some gas," he said. "This thing will move."

The El Camino jerked onto the road. My grandfather stuck his hand out the window and flapped it like a wing.

It was on the El Camino he taught me how to change a flat tire, how to jump a battery, how, most memorably, to siphon gasoline. He got down on his knees in the driveway. There was a red gas cannister beside him. He slid one end of a plastic tube into the car's open tank. He held the other end to his lips. He sucked hard and took a breath, sucked hard and breathed again. There was so much dread, so much revulsion in his quick strong pulls.

The whole time he was sucking, he was bracing for what was coming, steeling himself for the vile gusher already on its way, and when the gas finally hit his mouth, he spit violently, wretchedly, like Rooster Cogburn extracting venom from Maddie Ross's hand, but not before directing the tube into the cannister, which sloshed and grew heavy with gasoline.

When would you need to use a siphon? Hardly ever. When you're out of fuel in a parking lot somewhere without recourse to a service station. When your only option is to filch from another vehicle. The improbability was the point. The lesson was like a prophecy given to prevent its fulfillment. Knowing how to siphon gasoline minimized the likelihood of ever having to. Once you tasted the gas, you'd do just about anything not to taste it again.

His awareness of worst-case scenarios had its roots in a fear—present since childhood and reinforced by other near failures along the way—that his good fortune could be forfeited by lack of foresight and preparation. The possibility of ending up empty-handed kept his hands moving, full.

Once he told me about playing on a hillside with some kids from up the holler. When it came break time, his friends, all siblings but for my grandfather, and none of them babies anymore, lined up on the front porch where their mother sat broad-lapped in a chair, breasts exposed, ready to give suck. These memories haunted him as much as they humored him.

He could afford to eat out and buy produce at Piggly Wiggly, yet he insisted on putting out a big garden every year, even when he was wholly reliant on other people to plant, water, and pick it. Like the El Camino, he couldn't or wouldn't let the garden go. He lived on a hill ten miles north of Nashville. The soil around the house was mostly rock. The poor tiller bounced, banging down the jagged rows. There were bugs and weeds galore. Birds, rabbits, squirrels, racoons, and moles to contend with, and more sun than rain.

Driven by habit and by his stomach, but also by a kind of abiding paranoia, he was undeterred. He planted beans, peas, tomatoes, peppers, potatoes, turnips, lettuce, squash, pumpkins, cabbage, radishes, cucumbers. What if a war broke out? What if the markets crashed? Gas prices soared? What if drought turned into famine turned into food shortage? It had happened before, could happen again, and quicker than you think.

Weed-eating around his garden once, I was interrupted by a holler loud enough to hear over the revving of the motor and the whirring of the string. When I turned, my grandfather was storming toward me across the yard.

"Well, there goes our goddamn food," he said, motioning toward the trail of cuttings I'd left in my wake. Amid the grass, I'd mowed down a ring of marigold flowers, planted to ward off worms and other garden menaces. I'd mistaken them for wildflowers and weeds.

Several moments passed. He took out his comb. In his huff, his hair had fallen out of place. Now it was blowing around the top of his head like smoke. As he brushed it off his forehead and ears, he was transformed, his despondency and fury giving way to something like calm. He returned the comb to his pocket. He put his hand on my shoulder.

"We'll survive," he said.

I was the first grandchild. As such, the task fell on me to name him. His birth name was Virgil. It wasn't a family name. Nor was it given in homage to the poet. My great-grandparents had never read the *Aeneid*, the *Georgics*, the *Inferno*.

Even severed from the founding of Rome or a guided tour of the underworld, Virgil had gravitas. It sounded dignified, sort of epic. It was a touch mysterious. A name large enough to live into. They did not give him a middle name.

I called him Bub. The word came from a mispronunciation. We were buddies, that was what he said about us. When I tried to repeat him, "buddy" came out "bubby," which was soon enough shortened to Bub.

What did he think about the name? Did he push against it or encourage it? It must have been a little bracing, going from Virgil to Daddy (what my mother and uncle called him) to Bub. At least I hadn't called him Bubba. For better or worse, to his delight or disdain, the title took.

The name was unique, you had to give it that. Catchy, too, and with a pop. The *b*'s were important. They gave the name padding, rounding the edges, widening the berth. Written down, the word even sort of looked like him, a composed bulge, a sturdy corpulence kept delicately in check.

In time, he became Bub to all the other grandkids. At his funeral, some of his oldest friends even called him by the name. That I never referred to him as Grandpa Ray (what my mother had called Enos) or Granddaddy (what most of my buddies called theirs) was more of a lark than a matter of serendipity, and yet somehow, it's true, those names wouldn't have worked. We were too well acquainted for the ubiquitous remove those other titles implied.

For the first several years of my life, my father was working at a bank during the day and going to law school at night. My grandfather filled in, getting down on the floor with me, letting me play with his reading glasses and comb, toting me along for his morning chores, me in his right arm, a water hose or bowl of dog food in his left. When I cried at restaurants, which I was prone to do, little punk, he picked me up and walked me around, saying look-a-here, look-a-there.

We surveyed the bright fish in the tanks at the Golden Dragon. Fed crackers to the ducks around the lake behind Mallard's Cafe. He took me to the car and let me fool with the dials on the radio, one country station wheedling into the next. More often than not, he took his meal home in a to-go box.

Had he been like this with his own children? Was he remedying mistakes he'd made in the past? Had age focused him on what really mattered? Had my naming of him constituted a rebirth? These were questions for later. From my perspective, he had always been this way. Nothing he didn't know, nothing he couldn't do. Old, wise, and plenty active. So I named him Bub, and he named the rest. The lights in the sky were stars. The trees with stars for leaves were maples. The trees with knives for leaves were hollies. The white box on the pole out front? That was a martin house. The red box out back? That was a barn.

When I could sit without falling, he'd set me on the fence-post while he forked hay and rolled out new salt blocks for the horses, the names of which were beautiful and illustrative: "Fancy" after the Reba McIntire song, "Skip" for the wild hitch in his trot, "Misty Dawn" for the black-and-white swirl of her skin.

He was a blur of motion in the barnyard with the sun rising and falling behind him, with the hay dust floating in the air and the animals harking to his whistles and clicks, and me straining to see him and hear him as I'm doing now.

╭━━━

What will you remember most about him? I might have said his voice. How full it was of itself. How it was leavened with the genuine thrill of expression. How he would keep talking through laughter, his words riding his airy guffaws in waves.

How groggy it was in the morning, and how welcome to hear on the other end of the phone—*Drew boy, how you doing, son?* How it was an instrument he played as sure as Enos clawed the banjo, as sure as his mother hummed her Baptist hymns.

He was no singer, that was for sure. He wasn't even that much of a music fan. In his car, at a low murmur, it was mostly talk radio. Concerts were lost on him. If he'd had a record collection, he'd forgotten where it went.

By virtue of growing up in America in the mid-twentieth century, he must have known some Elvis and Jerry Lee Lewis, a Supremes' chorus, the standard Sinatra or two, but he could not tell you the difference between the Beach Boys and the Stones. Neither Beethoven nor James Brown was among his concerns.

What he had was a cache of old country songs: "Tear in My Beer," "Hello Walls," "You Are My Sunshine," "Six Days on the Road," "If You've Got the Money." In the mornings, as he readied himself for work, he sang about walking the floor and the moon being blue. He sang about trains, about whiskey glasses, about cheating hearts.

His singing was low and tremulous, part standing bass, part electric fence. That few ever heard it and even fewer praised it was no restraint, even when, as was often the case, his voice was freighted with the residue of the previous night's talk and whisky. He might pause to brush his teeth, pause to cheek another tobacco plug, then he would unpause and have at it again.

Like the course of his razor, like the swoop of his comb, his singing was a gesture of habit, autopiloted, almost incantatory. He sang choruses mostly. He'd hum vague verses until he landed at familiar lines. "On the road again / Just can't wait to get on the road again." "Oh my darling, Clementine." "Always late with your kisses, / Why oh why do you want to do me this way."

His half-possession of these songs—and theirs of him—had the effect of turning his whole routine into a kind of melody, even as it hitched the music firmly to the palpable, making it as real and mundane and every bit as practical as his comb and the back pocket he dropped it into.

For all their rawness, for all his apparent nonchalance, his selections seldom struck me as random. They might have been separated from him by a century, might have evoked, as in the case of "Clementine," a prairie dotted with cattle and tumbleweeds, or offered praise to asphalt and open road like the "Shotgun Willie" standard, and yet somehow each seemed of a piece with the old man. Beyond porch and garden, fencerow and toolshed, the woods around his place really were something of a wilderness, even if, in the winter months, you could see through them clear to neon Nashville.

"On the road again." The lyric strikes me now as pure incitement, like a first cup of coffee, a morning smoke, as if in singing it he had a mind to revving himself up for the day ahead, a day that would, no doubt, involve a great deal of driving, his business being cars, his customers spread across town, but in his mercurial rendering, benign and grizzled, the charge was tempered by a weary resolve. It was "on the road," as in, "time to get going." It was also "here we go, for about the billionth time."

Breathier now, more bruised, interrupted by longer silences, the songs trailed him from the bathroom to the kitchen and through the kitchen to the porch to where he toed into boots and hit the screen door to make his slow way across the yard and into the noise of slid latches, swung gates, and slung buckets, the racket of his morning rounds rising and falling around his whistling and still fainter grunts.

Whatever his singing lacked, his speech supplied. When he talked, his voice grew louder, more confident. The mountain accent in which his parents conversed—the strange diphthongs that turned *leg* to *lag*, the *r* that would insert itself where it didn't belong, making a *warsh* of *wash*—had, on my grandfather's tongue, been subsumed into a more lyrical, more distinctly southern brogue, part bullfrog, part bullfinch, heaven to listen to.

He loved to talk. It was as if the world presented itself principally as material for speech. No experience was complete until it had been said out loud, then said again. When he opened his mouth, it was as if he were greeting an old friend. Whatever else had come and gone into and out of his life, his voice had been with him from the start. It bent sound and silence into shape. It decelerated conversation—and seemed to dignify it, too.

Would his voice have worked on the radio? If it could have been harnessed and applied to a tight script, sure. In practice, though, no way. His speaking was too spontaneous, too used to moving at its own speed. It was responsive, above all, to the moment at hand. Like his family photographs—*don't pose, act natural*—his talk arose extempore. This would lead to that would lead to nowhere expected. Every instance had the potential to hang and hold open a gate in time.

Enos's side of the family was part Cherokee, and when my grandfather told a story, staring off into the distance as if summoning happenstance from up over the hillside, his alert face in profile, he looked regal. Shave his mustache, put hoops in his ears and a feather in his hair, and he could have posed for Edward Curtis in one of those slightly blurred, sepia-toned portraits from the previous century.

Among my favorite stories he told was the one about the

mule. They kept the animal in a shed off the side of the house. For all his charms, the mule was a local scourge, busting through fences, foraging in gardens, and so forth. One morning, after the mule had taken a particularly destructive pass through a neighbor's shed, his father said he'd had enough. That very day, he was going to put the mule down.

My grandfather volunteered to do it instead. One of his younger brothers delighted in torturing animals. He'd catch a stray cat and stick a piece of wood covered in turpentine up its ass. He'd tie a tin can to the end of the stick. When he lit the stick, the cat would zigzag across the yard, scared crazy by the burn and the blast. But when my grandfather pressed his rifle against the mule's head that night, he could not bring himself to pull the trigger. He begged Enos to let him wait till the morning.

By dawn he had worked up the courage. He dressed and grabbed the gun and headed for the stable. When he got there, he saw the mule was gone. He searched the garden. He searched the neighbors' yards and the hillside behind the house. He wandered down the road to the mouth of the coal mine and then along the riverbank field.

When my grandfather returned to the house to inform his father, Enos told him a story of his own. It turned out that while my grandfather had been out looking, a man from the railroad company had come knocking on their door. He'd come to deliver bad news. There had been an accident overnight. A mule had wandered onto the tracks and been struck dead. The man had gathered from people in town that the mule had belonged to them.

He had come to bring an official apology. He said he knew it was a minor consolation and would by no means bring the animal back to life, but would they accept a check for six hundred dollars?

It was a trickster tale, the kind of thing you find in Aesop. Or was it? The first time I heard this story I sat wondering for a while what exactly I'd been told. Had my grandfather been rewarded or cheated for his crisis of conscience? Had the mule caught wind of the fate that awaited him and hauled tail? Had my great-grandfather been behind it all along? Six hundred dollars would have been a fortune to them at the time, a kind of jackpot. But if a mule was worth so much, why would Enos have been so quick to dispense with it?

There was no lesson at the end, there was only the story, which my grandfather never told the same way twice, adding and subtracting details, starting from a different point, coming at the events from another angle to see what he would find. That I didn't understand it didn't keep me from sharing it at school, subbing myself in for my grandfather and upping the compensation from $600 to $6,000. The teacher laughed at first but when I swore it was the God's honest truth, she marched me down the hall to see my mother, who also taught at the school and who in turn scolded me and told me to apologize to my teacher, who in turn asked me to apologize to the class.

School, it seemed to me, was the antithesis of my grandfather's porch. At school, you opened your mouth at your own risk. School was about what things meant, not the way things really were. Explanations were prized over descriptions. Stories were scrutinized rather than enjoyed. Little wonder my grandfather and his friends had not gotten very far in school.

Still, the porch provided nothing if not an education. On weekend nights, they commenced a narrative free-for-all, one story leading to another, with jokes and banter thrown in between. It was a kind of jam session, unrehearsed yet seamless. They played off each other so studiously, listening until there came a point when they glanced away, shifted in their seat, or maybe pressed their lips together, and this meant that another story had occurred to them, and then they wobbled and rocked and sat back in their chairs, waiting for the chance to break in before the next guy began, and if it so happened that they missed their chance, they would grow quiet and maybe stand up and light a cigarette and look out through the screen into the shadows and trees until something in the story on offer captured their attention, and then they would laugh and nod and return to the circle as if in surrender. Some talked quickly, others with much affectation, their voices changing when they began to speak, their words clearer and more eloquent than they were in other contexts, but also possessed of a kind of wonder at what they might find such that they came across like actors reciting lines they couldn't believe they still knew by heart.

Like Homer and other figures from my grandfather's life, I knew these men as names from stories before I knew their voices, faces, eyes. Fluker. Robert Earl. Salem the Jeweler. Big Ern. Dr. DeLeon. When I met them in the flesh, on the porch or perhaps at my grandfather's office, it was like meeting figures from books. They had the distinctive, heightened-from-life quality of fictional characters. Their faces were like masks of faces, wrinkled, slightly swollen, weathered from sun and strain.

Twisted into grimaces or balled up in anger, they would have frightened trick-or-treaters on Halloween. On the porch, though, nodding in agreement, stretched with laughter, or shaking in disbelief, they affected the visages of happy gods.

One had hands like bricks, rough and impenetrable. One worked as an auctioneer. One was missing a limb. He tucked the empty sleeve into his pants' waist. "Tell him 'bout your arm," my grandfather would urge him. He gave a different version every time. A panther had ripped it off. He'd lost it in the Korean War. He'd got it caught in a combine. Trapped in a coal mine, he'd had to eat it to survive.

One with a handlebar mustache and a TCB necklace he'd received as a present from Elvis himself and whose obituary appeared in the *New York Times* when he passed away, told of the songs he'd written ("A Good Year for the Roses," "T-R-O-U-B-L-E") and the fish he'd caught. They talked about horses they'd broken and pranks they'd played. My uncle, who'd had front-row access to these rituals since boyhood and had become an ace raconteur in his own right, regaled the table with stories from the road.

The screen around the porch separated it, however porously, from the weather and the wilderness. It let in the breeze and the din of the southern night. It shielded you from the worst of the bugs and the rain while still letting you feel the world on your skin. Not quite in place, not quite out of place either, it was the kind of place Bub felt comfortable holding court.

We lived a quarter of a mile from my grandparents, on Moncrief Avenue, in the hills north of Nashville. On Friday nights my grandmother fixed a big supper, then we slept over so we could visit and work around the place on Saturday, mowing grass, stacking hay bales, watering animals, patching fence.

When I was old enough to stay up with the adults after supper, I sat in the corner of the porch in a rocking chair, listening. In the woods around the porch crickets and bullfrogs raised a wild ruckus. The winds wrestled in the tall trees. The chimes hanging around the porch screen made a watery music. The world outside was dark and loud and utterly oblivious to us, and yet there was my grandfather and his friends, alive and talking as if their lives were worth talking about, using words that had a resonance all out of proportion to their sound.

What I remember is heaviness, intensity, a state of heightened awareness that made my mind reel and my cheeks ache. In silence, I strained to hear every word, somehow envying the experience I was already having, already short for time while still in the thick of it. Later, I would read about how Kris Kristofferson swept floors at Columbia Records just to catch glimpses of Johnny Cash and Bob Dylan in the studio, about how Walt Whitman observed President Lincoln's commutes to and from the White House, and I recognized something of their desperate commitment in my own dedication to the storytellers on the porch.

One night, my younger cousins, who'd been sent off to bed after dinner, came tugging at my shirt sleeve, saying they'd heard a coyote from their bedroom and they were scared. I shooed them away, not wanting to have my revelry interrupted, and when they returned a few minutes later, I did the same, telling them to grow up and pushing them back through the door. The third time, my uncle, their father, intercepted them before they could get to me.

He knelt to eye level. "What's wrong, boys?" he asked.

They told him about the coyote. I was sure he was going to tell them there was nothing to be worried about and then send them back to bed, perhaps with a warning not to leave the bedroom again. Instead, he asked them to point to where they'd heard the sound coming from. They were taken aback. Tentatively, they pointed in the direction of the fruit trees. "There?" he said, pointing after them. They nodded their yes.

"Stay here," my uncle said, rising and turning for the screen door.

What was happening? Why was he interrupting the storytelling? It was as if Michael Jordan had checked out of a game at a crucial moment to address some minor skirmish in the stands.

My uncle walked across the driveway to his pickup truck. From a box in the bed, he lifted a rifle. By this point the others had caught wind of the disturbance. In the pens down the hillside, the beagles erupted. Spotting my cousins, who were still hunched together by my chair, my grandfather called them over, and they told him about the coyote.

Everyone watched as my uncle fired one shot and then another. The blasts were deafening but for their own echoes, which rolled over the din of night in waves. He placed the gun in the truck and returned to the porch. "That coyote won't be bothering you no more," he told my cousins. Then he asked me to take them back to bed.

I fell asleep that night looking at the lit porch through the bedroom window, thinking about the stories I wasn't hearing because of my scaredy-cat cousins, who lay in the bed beside me, already asleep.

The next morning, my grandmother asked me to collect some pears from the orchard. She was going to fry them for breakfast. I grabbed a bucket from the garage and headed outside. I salvaged what I could of the pears that had fallen to the ground, tossed the bruised and bug-gored ones under the fence for the horses. Others I picked from low-hanging branches.

My bucket was about half full when I began to smell something awful in the fruit trees. The deeper I ambled the stronger the stench. Then at the base of one of the apples trees, I saw a clump of what looked like fur. I set the bucket down and climbed up inside. There on a low branch was a coyote, shot through the side. But it was more alive to me than it had ever been before. I jumped out of the tree and, stumbling, ran as fast as I could for the house. When my grandmother asked about the pears, I said, "You won't believe..."

It was the first story of my own I remember telling. The fact was not lost on me that if my uncle had done what I'd wanted him to do, I wouldn't have had a word to say. To me, the stories told on the porch were central. To them, the stories were secondary to the life the stories described. They were always interruptible. They were the opposite of precious. They were discardable because they were liable, even likely, to be replaced by another.

But you couldn't go searching for material. You couldn't manufacture it either. The trick, if there was one, was to cultivate an openness to what was already there. What distinguished storytellers from the pack was apparent. To the storyteller, every uttered experience was capable of surprise.

To the end my grandfather loved to talk. In a recording I made not long before he died, his voice is weak. The pain in his body caused by congenital heart failure and complications from a second hip replacement surgery have been temporarily allayed by many medicines and steady swills of J&B. He's sloshed, in other words, and yet his voice, even this ember where the fire had been, is unmistakable. Sitting up in bed, tobacco spit dripping down his chin, he told me a story I'd never heard.

"This son and his father," he said, "his father had started this business, a big company, hundreds of employees, and his son talked to this college friend of his, and unbeknownst to the son, he was a hit man. So he said, 'Well, I can get that taken care of.' He said, 'I'm going to let him shoot me. And you and I will be the only two that know.' He said, 'I've got this shield and you can't shoot a bullet through it. It's heavy and it covers my whole chest. And I'm going to set an appointment with him. I'm going to go over to this park at 9 p.m. when nobody's there. He's going to shoot me and I'm going to fall just like I'm dead. When he leaves, you come and get me and call an ambulance, and they'll take me to the hospital. I've already set it up with the guy at the morgue, who will pronounce me dead. I'll be on a plane for wherever, and he'll admit to shooting me and he'll serve time in prison. I've already talked to your friend in the office, and he'll send you money every week if you just keep in touch with me, and you, under your contract with your dad, will have full control of that company. You won't be able to go out and show yourself, but you'll get paid, and when the time is right, you can come back.'"

"Now," he said, "can you believe that?"

"That's the craziest thing I've ever heard," I said. "Now, who are these people you're talking about?"

Turned out they weren't characters from his business dealings, from his childhood, or even from the newspaper, which the neighbors retrieved from the bottom of the hill and left on the porch for him each morning. They were actors in a soap opera he'd taken to watching in the middle of the day.

His wide world had been constrained to bed and bathroom, sleep and rest, and calling for my grandmother when he needed to take his pills, but his impulse to narrate what passed before his eyes was undiminished.

He laughed. "I got interested in that," he said, "and I thought, 'Now, how is this going to work out?'"

His getup was memorable. Did he own a pair of shorts? A pair of sweatpants or jeans? Certainly, T-shirts were never a staple of his attire. Except for the white undershirts and briefs he donned on the porch on summer nights late, his wardrobe was rarely less casual than a short-sleeved button-down with khaki slacks belted over, not below, his considerable paunch.

He dressed up to leave the house, dressed up more than most when he was housebound. His bedroom closet was over-stuffed with blazers, cuffed slacks, dress shirts, suits from McPherson's, suspenders, ties in every color imaginable, and enough belts, so it seemed to me, to ring the waists of every other biped in Davidson County.

No doubt the expansiveness of his wardrobe had to do with fluctuations in his weight. He'd go from 275 to 250 to back up near 300 depending on the medications he was taking and the diet he was on. Pants that fit one year didn't fit the next, and yet, because they might fit again in another year or two, he kept them, kept most everything, until there was hardly anywhere left to keep it all, the attic filling with boxes, the subdivided garage no longer housing cars.

Hats were an obsession. The branches of the coatrack in the laundry room were heavy with homburgs, panamas, boaters, fedoras. Nor was a cowboy hat ever far from reach. Some were leather, some canvas, others straw. I'd grab one to mow the grass or, later on, to bushhog the front field, and at first I felt like an imposter—his hats not crowning so much as devouring my head—but by the time I last-lapped the pasture and headed for the house, all the sweat the band had absorbed and the sunlight the bill had blocked had reconciled me, by and by, to the hat's occasional twist and wobble. I felt naked, I felt a foot shorter when I returned it to the rack.

Over the course of his adult life, he accumulated innumerable pairs of shoes. Shiny beneath a skein of dust, his oxfords and loafers, each lined with extra insoles to support his flat feet, occupied a long rack by the stairs. He kept pairs of boots on the porch, more pairs by the back door. It was not until the final years of his life, when his feet swelled with fluid and his legs lolled behind a walker that was eventually replaced by a wheelchair, that he capitulated to wearing sneakers he could slip on without the aid of a shoehorn.

Once, he even tried his hand at selling shoes. A storefront came open in a small retail space he'd purchased on Dickerson Road in North Nashville. He was having trouble finding tenants, so he moved several tall metal racks into the space and filled them top to bottom with pairs he'd purchased who knows where. My mother and grandmother took turns running the register while Bub and I worked the floor. The business lasted no more than a couple of months, but the local paper took an interest. They put my picture under the headline. Bub had called the store "Drew's Shoes."

When I turned seventeen, my grandfather took me across town to pick out a suit at McPherson's, the men's shop on Charlotte Pike with the green-and-white awning over the door. The one we bought was navy. The thread mixed cotton and polyester. The pants were pleated and cuffed at the bottom. The legs swayed when you walked. The jacket had two buttons, a single vent.

It was an old man's suit, but I didn't know the difference.

The in-house tailor took my measurements, making white markings in chalk. While we waited, Bub took me to lunch at Sylvan Park, a nearby meat and three. The country singer Eddy Arnold, a Sylvan Park regular, was sitting in a booth by the window. On record, Arnold yodeled about calling cattle across endless pasture, but like my grandfather, he was more comfortable in dress pants than denim. "Getting my grandson here his first suit," Bub said as we passed. "Pick me up one, too," Arnold shot back.

The suit was bagged and ready when we returned. The attendant had even thrown in a red necktie. In the near term, I had no occasion to sport my new threads. The Metro employees at the DMV, where I was working that summer, dressed business casual, and not even the county clerk wore a tie except in the one framed picture of him hanging on the wall next to the mayor.

But when time came for me to graduate high school, I wore the suit beneath my robe, and then when my first job in college required dressing up, I wore the thing three afternoons a week for two semesters straight.

Over time, sweat marks began to mottle the armpits. The breast pocket grew slack from holding a tape recorder and notepad (I was reporting on politics for the college paper from the state house). Through a hole in the jacket pocket, pens dropped into the flaps and slid around. To extract them from the lining required focus and luck.

I dropped the suit at the dry cleaners for the first time right before my college graduation. It had been five or six years since my grandfather bought it for me. As we posed for pictures after the ceremony, Bub said, "Now that's a good-looking suit right there."

"You're the one picked it out," I said.

"Well, what do you know about that?" he replied. "I guess you can't hide taste."

As much pride as he took in his clothes, he took as much pleasure in complimenting others. Seeing you in a shirt or sweater he fancied, he'd mention how it drew out your eyes or paired well with your coat. Sometimes, he'd go so far as to retreat to his closet and return with an item, maybe a vest, maybe an oxford shirt. He'd hold it up to you. "That's sharp," he'd say. "It's yours if you want it."

But his clothes weren't easily transferable. His shape was singular. He was big-stomached, thick-necked, slump-shouldered, short-armed. Untucked, without a belly to cover, his shirttails might fall all the way to your knees. But the cuffs would barely cover your forearms. To wear the shirts he gave me through the years, which I don't much, I have to leave the sleeves unbuttoned and give them a couple of rolls.

For his part, he looked extra sharp in a burgundy shirt with khaki slacks, brown socks, and two-tone derbies in tan and blue. It's what he's wearing in a picture taken by my grandmother when I was four or five. We're sitting in foldout chairs by a pond in the fall, leaves all around us, a campfire burning near out feet.

The burgundy, it magnifies the deep blue of his eyes, turns them almost violet. And the shoes, they're an unexpected match for the brown plaid blazer draped over his chairback. You like the blazer? I can almost hear him saying. Here, why don't you try it on?

Still, I might have said his presence. His aura. The shadow he cast. The penumbra that silhouetted us against his earthy radiance. How knowing he was up on the hill was a stay against a certain kind of listlessness, despair. How would it have been without him? Would we have ended up dead or broke or in prison? Who can say what disasters were prevented just by virtue of his being there?

Yes, and how there were times when his presence was overwhelming, when I wanted to buck the gravitational pull he exerted over my life and free float out of his radius, scared of what I might find, but needing, nevertheless, to see for myself.

Before I left for college, he pulled me aside. "I took us out of the coal mines," he said, his hands on my shoulders, "you take us from here." It was a beautiful encouragement, almost a benediction, an utterly original parting phrase. I ran the words over and over and over in my head. The more I considered them, the more confused I became.

What did he mean, "take us from here"? Where was "here"— Nashville? If so, what place did he have in mind? And who was "us"? Was I supposed to pack up the family and head for LA, like the hillbillies on the TV show? Was he talking about money? Thinking in terms of scale? He had grown up in a holler. He'd settled on a hilltop. Was the next station supposed to be a mansion on a mountain somewhere out West?

His hopes for me, I suspected, were mislaid. I loved the old man, couldn't stand the thought of failing him, but I had already begun to realize that I was nothing like him. I had never had his steady hands or his sure way with words. Nor would his business, his life's work, have been successful in my charge. But if I wasn't cut out for the family business, what was I cut out for? Nothing lucrative as far as I could tell. Mowing grass? Playing shirts and skins on the hardcourt at the First Baptist church? Scouring the Blockbuster by the Piggly Wiggly for films with subtitles?

I had started filling notebooks with poems, lyrics, and sketches. For Christmas one year, I typed up some lines, framed the sheet of paper, and gave it to Bub for a present. He read the poem and thanked me, but I could tell he didn't know what to say. Later that day, when his songwriter friend came over for Christmas dinner, I was surprised when he handed the frame to him and pointed in my direction. He didn't get it, he never would, but he knew someone who might.

"You take us from here," that's what my grandfather had told me. It wasn't all he said. The sentence was contingent on the one that preceded it: "I took us out of the coal mines." And so he had, and his doing so must have perplexed his family at every turn. His venture must have seemed riskier, far more reckless, than any trek Enos made into the mine. Lord only knows the worried prayers his mother had prayed.

No one could tell Bub what to do. He was stubborn as hell,

and if the road out of coal country was freighted with repos and long drives and rifle fire, well, that was the tax required for his recalcitrance. It struck me that doing like Bub could mean doing what Bub couldn't conceive of, that maybe living up to his expectation meant letting him down.

Whatever I did with my life would almost certainly seem benign by comparison. Instead of a narrative of ascent, mine would likely involve stasis if not decline. Still, he'd handed me reins that did not exist, but which, like the turning of his ear in the car all those years before, I received. *You take us from here.* Your turn now.

One morning, coming out of a meeting in DC, I got a call from my grandfather. I had not been expecting it. We no longer talked on the phone very often. Growing up, it had been the odd day that passed without a visit. Now years blurred by with no more than a check-in or two.

When I did drop by, on holidays, en route to elsewhere, he seemed untouched by time, selfsame, as old as he'd always been. His white hair was a shade whiter. His mind was still strong. He was occupied with his garden, with his martin houses, with his life.

I thought about him all the time. Told stories about him to friends. I had moved to Washington to write for magazines. It was a place he knew nothing about, an experience he'd never had, and yet I heard his voice every time I began to type words of my own. He was still with me in some unreal but actual sense, even though we'd never been farther apart.

My mother was always getting onto me about not calling home. My grandfather said he understood. He had left home too. You can't live two places at the same time, he said. He was happy to talk when it happened. There was no use forcing it. Silence was anything but, he told me. It meant you were busy, up to something important. I knew he was combating his own guilt as much as my own.

But seeing his number now, I panicked. Something had to be wrong, something that couldn't wait. I rushed from my office building and leaned against a lamppost at the corner of Nineteenth and L.

"What's wrong, Bub?" I answered.

The street was loud with traffic. I finger-plugged my other ear.

"Not a thing, grandson," he said.

"You had me worried," I said. "What's on your mind?"

What he said next I couldn't have anticipated. He said he was getting baptized the following Sunday. He wanted to fly me home for the service.

I had not known my grandfather to be religious. The only time I'd seen him in church was for the funeral services of friends. Once, when my mother invited him to attend with her on Easter, he told her he'd already "been to church in his heart." It was a provocative thing to say, a touch mystical even. It was also a clever way of refusing her request. He had been to church already, why would he go again? Whether he was sincere or had concocted the sacrament for this very purpose was up for debate. Except toward TV preachers and evangelists, he wasn't angry toward religion; he was dismissive. He seemed to feel no need. What, I wondered, had caused him to take an interest now?

The following Saturday morning, he picked me up from the airport in his El Camino. I put my bag in the bed, opened the heavy door, and slipped into the seat beside him. As we drove home on sidewinding back roads that set my head spinning, as if for the first time, he filled me in.

A few weeks earlier, one of his closest friends had been diagnosed with terminal cancer. Doctors had given him weeks to live. In a bid to raise his spirits, my grandfather managed to talk him into coming fishing with him early one morning on Percy Priest Lake. They baited their hooks and readied their reels, but neither of them cast. Instead, they sat there, the boat gently rocking on the water, a silence like concrete hardening between them. According to my grandfather, they would have sat there for a lot longer had a voice not interrupted.

"Beg pardon," my grandfather asked, rising to his feet and easing to the edge of the boat. A ways off, a man in a kayak was floating in the water, the sun coming up behind his head. My grandfather squinted to try to make out his face but couldn't tell much about him other than that he was shirtless. His head was shaved.

"I asked," the man said, "whether you boys had caught anything."

"Not a thing," my grandfather said. The man whipped his kayak around, then turned it back, the splashes from his maneuverings slapping at the boat.

"I used to fish this lake every morning," the man continued.

"That so?" said my grandfather.

"I spent too much time out here," the man went on. "Let the important stuff get away. Long story short," he continued. "It took me getting sick to get my attention. I sold my boat and made things right with my family. That was ten years ago. But that's more than you wanted to know."

"You hearing this?" my grandfather asked his friend, who had sat up and turned to get a look at the man. When my grandfather turned back to the kayaker, he was already paddling away. He whipped back around to face them once more.

"I used to catch a lot of fish in a cove over this way," he said, motioning with his paddle for them to follow him around a bend.

The cove was surrounded by steep rocks all around. There was no easy way up or out. But when my grandfather turned into it a few minutes later, the stranger was nowhere to be seen. That night, my grandfather said, he couldn't sleep. He kept seeing the kayaker. He tried to remember his face, but he never got a clear look at it. Had the man even been there at all?

Bright and early the next morning, he called his friend, who would die a few weeks later. His wife answered.

"Did he tell you about yesterday?" my grandfather asked.

"Tell me about it?" she said. "He's been up all night. Said you two might have seen an angel on the water."

Bub said he didn't know about angels, but he knew what had happened wasn't like anything that had happened before.

That day, he took out the phone book and found the number of the church that used to host pancake breakfasts for the local Masonic lodge. The pastor listened to the story with great interest, then invited my grandfather to church. He went the very next Sunday. He went the Sunday after that. He was surprised to discover he enjoyed it.

"The only two things that bring me any pleasure anymore," he told me, "are church and a glass of whiskey, and neither one of them lasts long enough."

On the morning of the baptism, I sat next to my grandfather in the church. The sanctuary was two sections of pews, three rows deep. It seemed hotter inside than outside, and the outside temp, said the bank sign we'd passed on the way there, was north of ninety degrees.

The assembly was comprised of old women and a few families with armfuls of young children. Bub had come dressed in a suit. He was very still. Instead of singing during the hymns, he alternated between staring down at the hymnal, scanning the room, and wiping the sweat from his forehead with a handkerchief. I wondered whether he was having second thoughts, wondered if he was picturing what all this singing and praying and rubbing shoulders with people you might not choose to associate with in other contexts looked like from the outside, and yet the reverence in his bearing was undeniable. There was no hint of mockery or disdain. Whatever his doubts, he seemed to count it a great honor to be there, as if he knew, deep down, he didn't deserve to be.

What had happened to him out on the water? I thought of the story of Abraham in the book of Genesis. He's sitting out front of his tent, maybe napping, the text doesn't say, but it's conceivable—he's nearing a hundred by this stage, and the story takes place, as the writer puts it, in "the heat of the day." In any case, when Abraham comes to, three men are standing before him. And what's strange is that they don't introduce themselves. They don't need to. Abraham knows who they are. He bows before them. Feeds them a big meal. Even washes their feet.

In certain renderings of the account, of which there are myriad in art history, painters give the trio wings and halos. In Tiepolo's depiction, for instance, they hover above the ground. In Chagall's, they've morphed into doves. But there is nothing in the narrative to suggest they have the outward appearance of heavenly creatures. In fact, no one but Abraham treats them as anything other than strangers, and this seems to be the point: How Abraham can see what the rest of his camp cannot. How his experiences have readied him to receive angels.

At the end of the service, after a sermon about Jesus raising Lazarus from the dead, the pastor called my grandfather forward. I had in mind that phrase from Larkin, "a furious devout drench." I'd pictured white robes and a dunking in a pond. The pastor, however, simply scooped his hands into a red bowl by the pulpit and uncupped them over my grandfather's head.

The water stayed pooled there, flat and shiny in his hair, and it wasn't until Bub went for his handkerchief again that drops hit his face and darkened his shirt and tie. Suddenly, I was right back on his porch on a summer night when I was a kid. There was the sound of thunder, and then the bottom fell out. Rain drummed against the yard in great percussive waves. Without announcement, my grandfather stood up and walked into the house. When he returned, he had a bar of soap and a bottle of shampoo in his hands. In the yard, he stripped naked. His hair was plastered to his forehead. His white legs were shining.

I stripped and followed him through the screen door. He handed me the shampoo. I poured some in my hand and passed it back to him. The mud puddles at our feet filled with suds while on the porch my grandmother stood shaking her head, trying not to smile, and hollering, "You idiots, you'll catch cold."

Like that shower in the rain, the baptism felt both surprising and inevitable, if far less dramatic. When the pastor placed his hands on my grandfather's shoulder and prayed for him in front of the congregation, Bub bowed his head but did not close his eyes. It's possible he shed a tear, but it was hard, in that moment, to tell tears from the sweat and the affusion. And yet for its lack of affectation, the event seemed consonant with the spirit of my grandfather's religious experience, which was less like an exclamation mark than a period half erased, less an about-face than a slightly more tentative step in the same general direction.

As we drove home together, windows cracked, the radio a murmur beneath the buffeting wind, I had a palpable feeling not of déjà vu but of simultaneity, a sense that somehow, all at once, like an outer ripple around a widening ring, I was myself at every stage, the awed little boy and the returned grown man—and perhaps even somebody I'd yet to become, still with a ways to go, still being steered by my grandfather, but for how much longer, and where to?

There was in the baptism ritual, for all its spiritual uplift, a bracing undertow. Walking through the waters, my grandfather had acknowledged his mortality and forced me to acknowledge it. He might live forever with the saints in glory, but first he would have to go into the ground. Of course, I knew this, had in a sense been preparing for it all my life. Even resurrected Lazarus, as the preacher pointed out, died again. Still, the people who knew him, as well as the ones who only knew of him, must have wondered about that right up until the end, even after the end. In the first case, Jesus had left Lazarus in the grave for four days. In the second, it might very well have been the fifth day or the morning of the sixth that Martha and Mary and the family finally resigned themselves to the fact that Lazarus wasn't coming back, that Jesus, wherever he'd got off to after his own resurrection, wasn't just in the next town over, waiting, as he had been before, for the right time to head back over and weep his old friend into the light.

Maybe they never stopped wondering.

I will remember the ticks he pulled from the beagles' ears.

The salt he sprinkled on turnips.

The pie tin of breakfast scraps he set on the sill.

"A three-legged dog walks into a bar and says, 'I'm looking for the man that shot my paw.'"

A sneeze like a steam whistle blowing.

The sag of his weight on my shoulder climbing a stair.

How the auctioneers greeted him in the course of their chant—*Hi biddabuy, biddabuy, Hey Virg.*

Flattened grass, flashing silver, in the rearview mirror.

"If we had biscuits we could have country-ham biscuits if we had country ham."

He's buried in a cemetery off Dickerson Road. To get to his plot, you pass a stretch of graves marked "Music Row," where Hawkshaw Hawkins, who died in the same plane crash that killed Patsy Cline, and Lefty Frizzell, among others, are laid to rest. On Lefty's grave marker there's an engraved flat-top Gibson guitar, the kind he made famous in the 1950s, and, in big block letters, the title of one of his biggest hits, "I Love You a Thousand Ways."

A thousand ways, that's how I'll remember him. Not as he was, as he was to me. Grandfathers are living myths. Their stature is the earned fruit of surviving. They collapse distance. They warp time. They give their ears, their apple peels, their odd abiding blessings. They go on ahead of us, on up the road, and then the road turns.

"You know," he told me before he died, "you meet different people throughout your life, and some of them you remember and some of them you don't."

"Hard to understand why," I replied.

"It's almost like the ones you don't remember, they don't count," he said.

"And even the ones you do remember, sometimes you're mixing memories."

"Well, take it from me, it gets worse."

"Seems like the first memories, though, those are some of the last ones to go."

"You never do forget them," he said. "They keep coming back."

MORNING WAVES

On a sunless morning in early September, twenty-some miles north of Charleston proper, I left my wife in bed, dressed my son in swimming trunks, and walked out the back of a rented condo for the Atlantic shore. Beckett had recently begun speaking in discernible English. At the sight of the seascape, he jolted up straight from his perch atop my shoulders and, in a fit of recognition, drummed his bare feet against my bare chest. Boat, he said. He leveled his left middle finger at a trawler on the horizon. Beach, he said, a little quieter. Sand.

I paused at the end of the boardwalk. A pair of terns downdrifted like kites in the breeze. The rap of Beckett's legs had slowed to a tapping. And what else, I asked, brushing at his toes. What else do you see? Ocean, he said, trailing off, as if he had found the word (learned from picture books in our DC apartment) a faulty measure of the real thing. Or perhaps he was bored. Or going in his diaper. The boy's reticence could make for a difficult read.

Once I hauled him to a Joan Miró exhibition in the National Gallery. I thought he might get a rise out of Miró's paintings of Catalan farmers. His favorite toy was a plastic barn. One of his first words had been tractor. I sidled up close to a large canvas called *The Farm*, the one that had hung over Hemingway's dining room table in Cuba before the revolution. I turned sideways to give Beckett a clear view of the lizards between the bean hills. He was statue-still. He was paying close attention. Or so I thought. His weight shifted, a slumping there at the center, and when I glanced down at him in the carrier, the drool was already pooling in the tucks of his neck.

Unlike the Miró, the beach seemed to rouse him. He heeled at my chest and pitched face forward. I had no sooner flipped

49

him from my back and stood him in the sand than he ducked my handhold and took off. Beckett had started walking around the time he started talking. He still staggered, still fell, still gave hell to his palms and knees, but a little less so every day and every day with quicker rebound.

He was nearly to the water before I caught him. When I offered my hand this time, he took it. I shot a look over my shoulder at the hotel balconies. For a moment, the thought of someone spotting us flooded me with anxiety. The clasp was one of those moves that outed me as a father, a title I still felt unfit to claim. Father was what my father was, what my grandfather was. Most days, I felt like a middle schooler headed to a dance in one of their old blazers, strutting but failing to look the part.

Daddy, Beckett said. He yanked at my arm and, when he had my attention, cocked his free middle finger at the fishing boat from before. (Where did he pick up this gesture?) It was in motion now, headed south toward Charleston, nicking a white ramifying gash in the outer blue. The beach was empty. A quarter to seven and not another shadow on that stretch of ash-gray sand. I wondered whether Beckett would go any farther. His introduction to the sea—six, maybe seven, months earlier—had ended in a mouthful of seaweed and a fit for the ages. My wife, half-joking, half-serious, worried that the incident had scarred him forever. He would never be able to fish or swim or make transatlantic flights. He would never be able to stomach *Treasure Island* or *Moby-Dick*.

But if Beckett had put to memory the earlier fiasco, he gave few signs. He flashed a sideways grin and marched with me into the shallows, dropped my hand and went splashing into the ripples and foam. He was still moving, yipping and kicking up spray, when a low, late-breaking whitecap sat him in the water. Before the next wave could crash, I scooped him into my arms. He was breathless, tense. I had a mind to call it a morning, but when I asked him whether he wanted to keep going, he nodded his head yes.

We waded into waist-high water. Beckett took hold of my neck. I bent my knees and dipped until our upper bodies were enveloped. It had been several minutes since I had faced the shore. I was under the illusion that we had been moving in more or less a straight line, but we had drifted a good ways from the boardwalk, rerouted, almost imperceptibly, by the tide. I pointed out the condo, the car, the pool, over which a crescent moon and palmetto tree slunk and whipped against a tall metal pole.

Just then, I noticed two women walking on the beach. They were lugging buckets, the shell-collecting kind, but they had ceased their foraging and were waving in our direction. I had never seen them before. Perhaps, I thought, they were simply being convivial, responding in kind to the sight of a father playing in the ocean with his son. In their presence, my insecurity shape-shifted into something like pride. I gave a harried wave, then spun around and lunged several long steps forward. The slime gave beneath my toes, and I felt a cold undercurrent on my calves.

Still, Beckett held on, even while the water lapped at our armpits. He was relying on me utterly. He had surrendered something of himself out there where his feet no longer touched bottom. Overcome by the trust in his hold, I dropped my hands to his middle and tossed him into the air. He shot from the water with splashes and gulps. At the top, a fraught look, the likes of which I had seen when he encountered big dogs, swelled in his eyes. But when I caught him and the spray cleared, he slapped at the water and shouted. *Again.*

"Again," I had learned, was Beckett-speak for bliss. "Again" was hard to inspire but easy enough to answer. In quick succession, I threw him into the sky one time after another, catching him at the waist just as his feet creased the water, sinking him chin deep before launching him yet again.

The water rained around us, sloshing and jetting, while the wind blinded and deafened me to our surroundings such that the cool wet ruckus, when it finally waned, was a kind of coming to, a returning to the senses, but not to stillness and not to quiet, for there were howls coming from the beach.

The pair from before was standing directly in front of us. They had dropped their buckets and taken to waving their arms in wide circles. I glanced over my shoulder to see whether I had missed something, to see if they were flagging down a jet ski or a snorkeler in the water beyond us. By the time I glanced back, they were jumping up and down. Hands cupped around her mouth, one of the women shouted urgent words I could not quite catch for Beckett's ardent cries of again, again.

I peered to my left and right but did not notice anything out of the ordinary, only waves under clouds and a kite tail of gulls drifting between. The fishing boat was but a glint now in the southern distance. Confounded and increasingly paranoid, I lifted Beckett to my shoulders and high-stepped through the waves and breakers, shifting him to my hip once I hit the swash.

The strangers ushered us onto the shore as if we had survived a shipwreck. One produced a towel and draped it around Beckett's shoulders. The other rubbed our backs and shook her head, asking if we were all right, repeating Oh God, Oh thank God.

The sprint to shore had sucked the breath out of me. What was it? I asked through gasps. What was it in the water? A fin, they said. They had seen a fin where we had been wading. Beckett slumped on my hip, dangling his arm like he wanted down. We thought we'd never get your attention, the women continued. We thought we were going to have to come in after you. The frightful word went unspoken: shark.

I stood Beckett in the sand beside me. I looked again but still saw nothing but sea. Was it out there? And if so, had we been in danger? The fin might very well have belonged to a dolphin. Even so, I couldn't shake the notion that I'd offended a tacit code of fatherhood. The first rule, the only rule: never put your child in harm's way. But when I bent down to check on Beckett and attempt to express my remorse, he was oblivious. He held up a frittered piece of driftwood. Stick, he said, and lifted it over his head like a torch. And for a flash that still flickers, it seemed that for all my failures, real or imagined, I had managed to shield him from something big while we were roughhousing in the water—from jaws perhaps, but also from my doubts, fears. What could come between us now? We had survived the morning waves.

IT'S STRANGE THE WAY
THE LORD DOES MOVE

The other night, up late again listening to old records, I came across a song by Lefty Frizzell that, so far as I know, I had never heard before. It was the title that got my attention: "There's No Food in This House." I imagined Lefty, in his most vexed falsetto, leveling the words at a cheating lover who, in a final act of defiance, blows the week's grocery money on a trip to the salon. He had other songs to this effect: "You're Humbuggin' Me," "Always Late (With Your Kisses)," "Run 'Em Off," "You Want Everything but Me." Merle Haggard called Lefty "the most unique thing to ever happen to country music." He was, among other things, a kind of hillbilly Falstaff, Nashville's great minstrel of aggrieved accusations.

Lefty was a leading figure in the country movement called honky-tonk, which adapted the genre—previously the province of barn dances, bandstands, and festivals—to the beer hall. Rock 'n' roll was an influence. Hollywood was too. Lefty's publicity photos for Columbia Records in the early fifties pretend to black-and-white film stills. In a classic shot from 1951, he wears a fringed Western shirt and a bandanna scarf, looking like Edward G. Robinson doing his best Davy Crockett.

Honky-tonk music could be scandalous. Heavy drinking and infidelity were recurring themes. Webb Pierce, one of Lefty's contemporaries, had big hits with "There Stands the Glass" and "Back Street Affair," one an ode to the cathartic powers of whiskey, the other a sentimental defense of sleeping around that prompted a response from Kitty Wells, the reigning queen of country music. "You didn't count the cost," she parried in "Paying for That Back Street Affair." "You gambled and I lost / Now I must pay with hours of deep despair."

To the pairing of bottle and bedroom, Lefty added a third member, the empty pocket. In his first chart-topping single, 1951's "If You've Got the Money (I've Got the Time)," he played a carousing cheapskate angling to paint the town ("We'll have fun, oh boy, oh boy") on his sugar mama's dime. In his last chart-topping single, 1964's "Saginaw, Michigan," he tells the story of a poor midwestern fisherman who, in a bid to win the blessing of his true love's father, travels to Alaska to pan for gold. The dig comes to nothing, but the fisherman is unwilling to concede defeat, and so he mails a letter back to Saginaw claiming "I hit the biggest strike in Klondike history." The father believes the lie, offers his daughter's hand and, having convinced his son-in-law to sell his Alaska claim, sets out to collect. "The greedy fool," Lefty sings in the smarting final verse, "is looking for the gold I never found." The new couple, meanwhile, becomes "the happiest man and wife" in the Midwest.

A rags-to-riches fantasia, "Saginaw" doesn't seem, on first listen, to fit with Lefty's songbook, an otherwise singular catalogue of pique and letdown. But the song is up to more than it announces. I don't think Lefty buys the message he's peddling for a second. The specious letter on which the narrative turns might just be an analogue for the song itself, only the intended recipient isn't a father looking to protect his daughter from life in the poorhouse but a listener looking to popular music for blessed assurance. It's as if Lefty is saying, I'll play you the mush you want to hear, but don't blame me if in the end your golden dreams about romance and riches come to sawdust.

Lefty used vocals to complicate lyrics rather than letting lyrics dictate the way he sang. A comparison to Hank Williams, the dean of honky-tonk singers, is apropos. Hank inflated his thin, tremulous voice to reify the emotional register of his songs. In "I'm So Lonesome I Could Cry" he sounds just so. In "(I Heard That) Lonesome Whistle," he taffy pulls the word *lonesome* into a lolling five-syllable yodel that manages to summon both a train and the hills through which its whistle blows. What Hank was after was candor. "You ask," he once told a reporter, "what makes our kind of music successful. I'll tell you. It can be explained in just one word: sincerity."

Lefty called sincerity into question. His subject wasn't candor so much as its projection. The dynamic even found expression in his name. Born William Orville Frizzell, Lefty picked up the moniker, so the story goes, boxing southpaw in south Arkansas, where his father worked in oil.

On stage, though, Lefty wasn't a lefty at all. He played a flat-top Gibson guitar with his right hand. The name attested to his craftiness as a performer, a characteristic that was refracted in his singing style. His thick voice stayed a touch punch-drunk with itself. It was an organ board of concomitant pitches. Lubricated, slightly esophageal, he sang like a man knowingly going through the motions. In his love songs, the results could be comical. Covered by Hank Snow or Jim Reeves, "I Love You a Thousand Ways," another early hit, could pass for a litany of sweet nothings. But Lefty, who wrote the song for his wife after getting caught fooling around, coos affirmations—"I'll be true," "Darling, you're the only one," "I'll love you every day"—with a voracity that evinces suspicion.

The same quality of connivance that kept Lefty's love songs from curdling and lent the ones about heartache their fortifying self-awareness is also present in "There's No Food in This House," though the subject matter couldn't be more different. For starters, there is no incredulous husband involved. Rather, the song, which appeared on the same album as "Saginaw, Michigan," is rendered from the perspective of a child. "Sister says she's hungry," the song begins. "Brother says he's hungry too / If daddy don't get a job real soon / I don't know what we're gonna do." The boy's age isn't given, but we gather he's too young to work, too young for school. Despite his youth, or perhaps because of it, he is undistracted. He knows his family is in trouble, that his father has been laid off, that the store has cut off their credit line, that the cupboards, never that full to begin with, are empty now.

Times have been hard, the boy says, for "two months and a day." The precision of the count stresses the severity of the dilemma as well as its merciless lag. A couple of months isn't all that long in the grand scheme of things, but you know right away what he's getting at—two months and a day might as well be forever.

"The aim of every artist," Faulkner said, "is to arrest motion, which is life." What moves the song is the boy's worried appraisal of his parents' reactions, the way his father seems to have given up hope, the way his mother is in denial. His older brother and sister are starving; as he discloses in the one-line chorus, "there's no food in this house."

In Lefty's handling, the chorus becomes a question masquerading as statement of fact. The narrator isn't confused about why the family can't afford groceries. That, he knows, has to do with his father's layoff. We suspect that even if the father's fortunes were to turn tomorrow, if he were to find a way to cobble together enough odd jobs to restock the shelves, the boy wouldn't be satisfied, not anymore.

It's as if he's started to wonder why unemployment and hunger should exist in the first place, as if he's begun to suspect that the human condition is one of want instead of comfort and that the ache in his belly points to a hole in the heart of things. In the final verse, when help does finally arrive in the form of a meal offered by neighbors from the local church, he is grateful yet wary. "It's strange," he says, "how the Lord does move."

In the decade after he recorded "There's No Food in This House," Lefty's health and career declined. He neglected his voice, succumbed to alcoholism, and fought with his record label, which cut him loose in 1972. He died from a stroke three years later, at the age of forty-seven.

For all their setbacks, Lefty's final years yielded beautiful songs. In "I Never Go around Mirrors," he rattles off the types of characters he can't stomach (unshaven men, men with wine on their breath) only to reveal, in one of the most chilling turns in country music, that the character he has in mind is Lefty Frizzell. Delivered in little more than a whisper, the song refuses his old honky-tonk shtick. Lefty collapses the knowing remove that marked his early work and embraces sincerity to devastating effect.

Unlike "I Never Go around Mirrors," "There's No Food in This House" isn't autobiographical. We have no reason to believe that Lefty was once the kid in the song. Still, it's not hard to imagine the kid growing up to become a man like Lefty: curious, undeluded, discontented in and out of love, never forgetting his hunger, never forfeiting his grievance, but wringing from each a genuine music that goes on moving because it is life.

SEEING RED

The wasp's quick, menacing, unpredictable stab. I am crouched beside the tire of a pickup truck in Tennessee, my fists balled around my already burning ears. It's a Saturday in the summer. On the tailgate, my grandfather, my uncle, and their crew of posthole diggers and concrete pourers have knocked off working for long enough to eat lunch: leftover biscuits, sliced tomatoes, boiled eggs.

I am nine years old, soon to be ten. When people ask me what I want to be when I grow up, I say "country singer," I say "Braves center fielder," but what I think I want to be is one of these men. I want to be tough like them, steady handed. The truth is I'm not sure I could be even if I tried. What I am is in thrall to them, which is to say afraid of making a fool of myself in front of them. At the moment, though, I am more afraid of the wasp.

What kind of meanness is a wasp? What kind of mistake? Even for flying bugs with stingers, of which there are legions in the hills north of Nashville, wasps seem severe. Sure, a bee can sting you, make you swell, but bees make honey, and besides, a bee will sting you just the once. Their lives tied to their weapon, they strike as a last stand, then leave their weapons behind as if offering concessions. Wasps show no such restraint. They are indiscriminate. They don't carry a weapon, they are the weapon, knives gone airborne, anger on wings.

By *wasp*, of course, I mean *Polistes carolina*, the red paper wasp. Called "paper" because their nests are papier-mâché globes of chewed-up leaves and tree bark. Called "red" for their color, though red doesn't quite nail it. Reddish-brown is closer, the color of corroded metal, perfect camo for sneak attacks on kids taking cover behind rusty bumpers and wheel wells. But red, red is the color they inspire. Red, that bright shade of hot fear.

I see wasps everywhere. See their great nests in high branches and hanging like cursed piñatas from the rafters in the barn. I watch them chewing through porch screens and crawling along the dusty dashes of cars. Even when I can't see them, I sense them—I know they're there. Later, I will read how James Baldwin learned from reading certain passages in Dickens that literature, even the best literature we have, isn't always to be trusted, and I will come to feel similarly about Romantic poetry generally and particularly about Wordsworth, who in all the many gorgeous lines he wrote about trees and fields and wildflowers waving in the sun, never once, to my knowledge, mentions wasps.

People will tell me wasps aren't aggressive. They'll swear that hornets, yellow jackets, and dirt daubers are more irritable. They'll say wasps won't bother you if you don't bother them, but I don't believe them any more than I believe Wordsworth. A couple of years earlier, I'd been stung while on a class trip, and I hadn't bothered the wasp in the slightest. I hadn't even seen it coming. One moment, I was laughing with friends, the next I was writhing in the grass. The attack felt personal, and, indeed, it was personal, for the wasp had stung me, of all places, on my left ear.

Sting aside, my ears were already a source of anxiety. Too large for my head, too large for any head really, they were liable, at any moment, to flush purple. From what I could gather, I'd inherited them from Homer, my grandmother's father. A coal miner in West Virginia, he died long before I was born, but I was startled by my likeness in black-and-white pictures of him from the forties and fifties. The framed one in my grandparents' back bedroom might as well have been a mirror. Like Homer's, my ears had something of the gramophone about them. It was as if in the womb, in an attempt to make out the music and muffled voices on the other side of our mothers' stomachs, we'd cupped our ears with such frequency and force that they'd set that way, all agog, on the sides of our heads.

Naturally, my ears were a target for older kids' flicks and finger thumps, but no thump had ever made them throb like the wasp. My eyes flooded with tears before I had the chance to stop them. One of the mothers who'd accompanied us on the trip came to my aid. She said she had a remedy. She pulled from her purse a bottled water and a pack of Virginia Slims. She sliced open a cigarette with her long fingernail, sprinkled water on the tobacco, and pressed the brown mash against my ear. The makeshift compress did relieve the burning, but when I returned to my friends, they eyed me with alarm. In the bathroom mirror, I saw why. My ear had taken on new dimensions. It wasn't an ear at all. It was a purple circus balloon blown up and twisted into an ear shape. It was hideous, that's what it was, and it stayed so for the length of the bus ride back to school.

But as much as the sting had hurt and humiliated me, it was the times I'd narrowly escaped getting stung that haunted me most. On the hill above my parents' place, there was a ruin of a burned-down mansion. The owners, the story went, had torched the pile on purpose, hoping to collect on the insurance. You could glean something of the house's former glory from the charred remains. Stone walls, crumbling in places, still surrounded much of the plot. Not only was the steep driveway paved, it was covered with a gabled roof, a flourish that proved doubly strategic, shielding the driveway from snow and ice in the winter while also barring fire trucks from the flames.

On the far side of the property, overlooking a series of smaller hills, there was a large swimming pool, which must have been heaven on earth in the summer, a middle finger thrown at the southern sun. A ragged tree grew up through the liner now. From the diving board, which creaked when you stepped on it but wasn't going anywhere, you could get hold of a branch and climb inside. What kind of tree was it? Not any kind you wanted in your yard. The leaves were coarse, pockmarked. You itched at the slightest brush of the bark. It seemed less like a tree than a hex in tree form, as if the land had rendered judgment for the arson by driving a stake into the pool's heart.

In any case, I was up in that tree one afternoon, when on the branch in front of me a little pod opened and out of the husk, as if birthed into being at that very moment, a red paper wasp bloomed buzzing. I lost my mind. I swatted and flailed and tumbled into the pool bed, which was full of broken beer bottles, old porn, love roses, twigs. Cut up and frantic, my sweaty arms crosshatched in blood, I high-stepped through the muck, making for the rusted ladder. Still, the wasp persisted. I swatted and swatted at it, and then I swatted at the specter of it until I arrived back at home. Somehow, I had escaped, but escape couldn't have felt any more futile. The wasp would be back. Maybe not that wasp, but some wasp would.

And now it's here, huge as ever, trigger-happy, hounding the truck. It's hovering over the truck bed, its stinger and legs suspended as if gathering intel on who to attack first and who next, and how many times and when. How no one else seems to notice, how the workers go right on eating and talking around the tailgate, beggars belief. For all I know, in a moment the wasp will land in my hair, crawl down my neck. I'll look down, my crossed eyes sliding into focus, and see the wasp on the tip of my nose. I'll feel it before I see it, and it will be too late.

I close my eyes and see nothing but red. I brace for the sting, the one that will lay me bare in front of my heroes. But suddenly, through my half-covered ears, I hear something unexpected: silence. All at once, the men on the tailgate have gone rock quiet. The whole world, it seems to me, is standing still. Cautious yet curious, keeping one eye out for the wasp,

I make my slow way around the truck to where the workers are circled up now, frozen.

There's an edge in the air I don't understand, a strange mix of nerves and mistrust and wonder. Has somebody been stung? I shoulder my way between my grandfather and my uncle, who moves his cigarette to his mouth and stands me in front of him. He bends down, motions forward. "Look a-there," he says. "Son, you won't believe."

In the middle of the circle stands a man named Fred. He's a mechanic, a carpenter. He sometimes sleeps in my uncle's barn. The year before, he had nearly lost a leg when the electric augur with which he'd been digging holes for a new fence-row had caught on his blue jeans and pulled him inside. He's shirtless now, sweating. His ball cap is pushed way back on his head, and between his thumb and middle finger, he's holding the wasp.

Has he pulled it out of the air? Charmed it like a snake? I step closer. The wasp is straining against his fingers. I can see the wings flexing, the stinger probing air and skin. The wasp wants to kill Fred, wants to kill all of us, but—I see now why the others are marveling—it can't get its stinger into Fred's hand. It prods again and again but can't find purchase. Calloused over from work, from the tools and the heat and the decades of roughness, his hands are impenetrable. The wasp might as well be trying to sting a stone wall.

In years to come, I will know worse pain than wasp stings, know deeper humiliation, far greater fear. I will know that the pain I feel is as nothing compared to the pain of others. Wasps, never pleasant, will nonetheless become part of the shit of life one accepts as a given, so much so that their absence in Wordsworth, let alone in all those country songs about summer, will make a kind of sense. To keep going you do have to ignore a lot.

At this moment, though, with the wasp between his fingers, before it falls to the grass and he finishes it off with his boot,

Fred might as well be holding sickness or poverty or war—just the worst thing you can think of—maybe sorrow, maybe death itself. And if a red paper wasp, a danger once so formidable, can be made to look this powerless, this small, then who's to say there's not a day coming when all those other devils lose their sting too?

VISIONS OF CASH

My grandmother tells a story about me and Johnny Cash. She was working as a receptionist at a bank off I-65, just north of Nashville. She'd taken me to the office with her one morning, letting me restock the countertop pens and peppermints, when Cash came in to make a deposit.

I was a painfully shy kid, so as Cash approached, I took cover the one place I could find, behind my grandmother's pant leg, shoulders slumping, face turning red. Cash bent down to eye level. We were standing near the brick entryway.

"And who is this young squire?" he asked.

My grandmother nudged me forward. "Go on, boy," she said. "Tell Mr. Cash your name."

I wouldn't say it.

"Go on," she repeated. "Tell him what to call you, now."

But still I wouldn't say.

Cash tousled my hair a little and then got on with his business. He was a regular at the bank. In the summers when she was in high school and college, my mother worked there too. Once, she'd been helping Johnny and June with their safety-deposit box when the heavy door latched shut behind them, locking them inside. From inside the vault, she'd had to call security. It took longer than it should have to get out. In a line that became a running joke between them, Cash said she'd have made a bad bank robber.

The one my grandmother tells ends like this: a few minutes later, Cash walked back across the lobby, waving. The wooden doors shut behind him and, as the doors shut, right at that very moment, as if forced from my mouth by the heavy sound, I finally said my name.

I have never known quite what to make of that story, which is a nonstory really, except that it involves Johnny Cash. Apparently, my tendency to say the right thing too late if at all goes back to earliest days. If nothing else, the story highlights the way Cash loomed over my childhood. I may not have taken the chance to give him my name, but I cannot recall a time when I didn't know his.

Cash. A single, steadying syllable, a buoy in a breaker, a banister on the ledge. In everyday usage the word meant hard money, and, to be sure, Cash did give off an air of reckless abundance, but he equally projected strength, integrity. You could count on Cash. He had never not been there. He was a landmark, fixed and orienting, more like Rose Hill or Old Hickory Lake than the old men in corner offices at my grandmother's bank. When you heard Cash's name or said it, you felt a mix of intimidation, safety, and intrigue. The name preceded and superseded its namesake, such that when you saw Cash in person, in the shape of a person, and realized that he was, in fact, a person, the encounter didn't quite register, at least not in real time.

In middle school, I had a friend named Cecilia who lived a few houses down from Cash, in Hendersonville. Cecilia's father was big in insurance. Word had it they had a roller-skating rink in their basement. One Saturday afternoon before a school dance, a group of us met at the house to pose for pictures with our dates. Before long, we had secured a football, shed our rented tuxedo jackets and, to the disdain of our mothers, commenced an impromptu game of two-hand touch. Up the driveway and into the street we spilled, handing off and lateraling, a Hail Mary pass overshooting its target, the ball skittering, side somersaulting, and coming to wobbly rest against the farther curb.

At some point, we were alerted to the approach of a vehicle. We turned. Coming toward us was a long black Cadillac, for which we cleared a haphazard path. Once the car had gone through, headed for the gated driveway at the bend in the road, we flailed into its wake, eager to get in as many downs as possible before the dance. Only later would the thought set in, "That was Johnny Cash."

Despite the ubiquity of his name in the hills north of Nashville, the man himself remained something of a cipher. His nearness created distance, his legend an obscuring fog. At some point, I assumed, never consciously, that I knew just about all there was to know about him and so, in truth, knew very little.

I remember a conversation with my mother the summer before my senior year of high school. At the time I was reading Kafka, listening to Ghostface Killah, and renting whatever foreign films I could find at the Blockbuster by the Piggly Wiggly on Gallatin Road. I had started wearing lots of black, even to church, and my parents, whose summer wardrobe consisted of various shades of khaki and white, were concerned.

After a couple of Sundays, my mother had had enough. She sat me down at the kitchen table and asked me what was wrong. Was I doing drugs? Was I depressed? It was summertime—wasn't I hot?

"Johnny Cash wears black," I said. "Do you have a problem with him?"

"Son," she said, trying her hardest not to laugh, "you're not Johnny Cash."

Cash dressed in black, she told me, to make a statement. He was drawing attention to the plight of poor folks, Vietnam vets, Native Americans, prisoners. What, she asked, was motivating my fashion choices?

I didn't have an answer, I wasn't sure I needed one, but I caught her meaning: there was more to Cash than I realized.

⌒

Whatever the length and substance of my familiarity with Cash's persona, of this I am certain: I was acquainted with his music first, even if I didn't know the music was his. In the mornings, my grandfather, as he readied himself for work, sang snatches of country songs. He was my first radio. There was no song he sang with more frequency than Cash's "Daddy Sang Bass."

"I remember when I was a lad," it started, "Times were hard and things were bad." And so they had been. My grandfather had grown up in Appalachia during the Great Depression. In his rendition, the song sounded less like a monster hit ("Daddy Sang Bass" stayed atop the Billboard country chart for six weeks in 1968) than a private reverie, maybe even a prayer.

"Daddy Sang Bass," at heart, is a song about survival. Grappling with the loss of his brother, the narrator finds succor in memories from a childhood that, for all its hardship ("Just poor people, that's all we were / Trying to make a living off of black land earth"), was leavened by music. "Daddy sang bass," the chorus goes,

> Mama sang tenor
> Me and little brother
> Would join right in there
> Singing seems to help a troubled soul

The last line is saving. The word "seems" manages to ransom the lyrics from pure nostalgia by conceding music's inability to totally redeem impoverishment and loss. Music, it says, can't ever really do anything but seem, but for as long as it plays, it makes seeming enough.

"Daddy Sang Bass" also offered a gloss on the history of country music. You expect the chorus to fade into a second verse. Instead, the song reaches back in time, roping into the mix, as if from out of nowhere, the hook from "Can the Circle Be Unbroken"—a song that Cash's in-laws, the legendary Carter Family, recorded in the 1930s, and which itself was an adaptation of a gospel song from the turn of the century.

"Can the Circle Be Unbroken" was one of the first country hits. It quickly became a Grand Ole Opry standard. In the process, the unbroken "circle" became a metaphor for country music in general, so much so that when the Grand Ole Opry moved from the Ryman Auditorium to the Grand Ole Opry House on the outskirts of Nashville, a move that signified country music's growing popularity, the stage featured a wooden circle salvaged from the old site.

The song's inclusion in "Daddy Sang Bass" isn't as arbitrary as it first appears. As the listener comes to realize, "Can the Circle Be Unbroken" is the very song the narrator remembers singing with his family. In this way, "Daddy Sang Bass" testifies to that older song's resonance, foregrounding its journey from Opry stage to radio waves to the living rooms and cars of a whole generation of listeners who possessed it, treasured it, like a shared understanding.

Musically, "Daddy Sang Bass" has more to do with Jerry Lee Lewis than Mother Maybelle. It was written by Cash's old Sun Records protégé Carl Perkins. A central figure in Memphis rockabilly, Perkins composed, among other hits, Elvis's "Blue Suede Shoes." Lyrically, however, "Daddy Sang Bass" is an unabashed throwback. In this way, the song transports the past into the present, as indeed my grandfather did when he sang the words all those mornings ago.

He wasn't much of a singer, but there never was a singer whose delight in the sound of his voice was more total. He took his razor, still dripping, for a microphone.

"Daddy sang bass," he started.

"Mama sang tenor," I answered.

Then together: "Singing seems to help a troubled soul."

Here's one I tell about Johnny Cash. I was in a bookstore perusing the magazine racks when one of the music rags caught my eye. The cover announced a list of the "greatest artists of all time." A sucker for lists, I dropped my backpack by the newsstand and flipped open the book.

There was Bob Dylan and Aretha Franklin. There was Elvis, Marvin Gaye, Madonna, the Rolling Stones. And, lo and behold, just a few pages in, there was Johnny Cash. Cash! The one who'd called me "young squire"? The one who lived down the street from Cecilia? I knew he was important, but I'd thought he was Nashville important, country-music important, important to my mother, important to my grandparents. I had not realized he mattered to people outside the circle. I had not realized how wide the circle really was.

It was 2003. I was a sophomore in college. I was living in a dorm room five hundred miles from home. Cash's album *The Man Comes Around* had just been released. Although several posthumous records would follow, it was the last album Cash would put out during his lifetime. *The Man Comes Around* is essentially a collection of bone-stripped covers. Guided by rap-rock producer Rick Rubin, the songs were sundry and eccentric. In their cockeyed way, they filled out and contextualized Cash's repertoire.

In "Sam Hall," the belligerent English folk ballad ("I killed a man, they said, an' I smashed in his head"), I sensed the spark for Cash's "Folsom Prison Blues" ("But I shot a man in Reno just to watch him die"). Likewise, Cash's sober version of Hank Williams's "I'm So Lonesome I Could Cry" felt like a pilgrimage back to the source. Other songs, Cash transmogrified. Depeche Mode's sensual "Personal Jesus," in Cash's handling, sounded less like a sexual entreaty than an altar call.

Even more miraculously, Cash managed to turn Nine Inch Nails' "Hurt," a jagged number about heroin addiction, into the last will and testament of an aging superstar. The original, as performed by Nails' front man Trent Reznor, was either a plea for help or a suicide note. Reznor's antic whisper in the dark was full of fear and self-loathing. Cash's version was wisdom literature, the book of Ecclesiastes ("Vanity of vanities; all is vanity") interpreted by a southern Lear.

Cash was declining in health, that much was clear. Once an elegant wail, his voice was ragged now, unrefined, and yet you sensed something urgent and essential in his delivery, however much it hurt. There was a searching quality to his singing. It was the musical equivalent of Rembrandt's late painting of the blind Simeon holding the newborn Christ. Cash's rough voice, like Rembrandt's shaky brush, possessed a fresh confidence in vulnerability. It moved like a chisel feeling old stone for truer shapes.

Not long after I bought *The Man Comes Around*, my mother called and told me that Cash had passed away. She said it matter-of-factly, but I could tell she was upset. June had died a few months earlier. He hadn't been the same since then, my mother said. "Still," she continued, "I think deep down I thought he would never die."

I knew what she was saying. This was two years after 9/11. Not since that day had I felt so disoriented. It was as if a fist had punched a hole in one of the world's load-bearing walls. The sky seemed to sag. The rope tying me to home, already fraying by that point, ripped a little and twisted. It was as if Rose Hill had slid into Old Hickory Lake.

The Man Comes Around ends with an irreverent cover of Vera Lynn's "We'll Meet Again," the World War II–era ballad: "We'll meet again / Don't know where / Don't know when / But I know we'll meet again some sunny day." The sunny day, in Lynn's starry-eyed take, is the armistice. In Cash's version, however, the sunny day is the song itself.

Cash is accompanied by what the liner notes call "the whole Cash gang." June is there, and so are the children, the grandchildren. In their unvarnished chorale, you can hear the fulfillment of the promises laid out in "Daddy Sang Bass." "I know we'll meet again," they sing, the dead and the still living, if not in harmony, in unison. No, the circle won't be broken, by and by, Lord, by and by.

A TAXONOMY OF COUNTRY BOYS

To be or not to be a country boy? To my ear, this has always been one of the animating questions in country music. In "Thank God I'm a Country Boy" (1974), John Denver, for instance, revels in the persona. From the picture he sketches, it's not hard to see why. Country boys, Denver says, have all they need: a warm bed, good work, regular meals, fiddle music. The life of a country boy, he sings, "ain't nothing but a funny, funny riddle," and who doesn't like a good laugh?

For Hank Williams Jr., however, this country boy business is no joke. In "A Country Boy Can Survive" (1981), he says the rivers are drying up and the stock market is anybody's guess and the world, as a general rule, is going to hell, and if you knew what was good for you, you'd be a country boy too, because in the end only country boys—the ones "raised on shotguns," the ones who know "how to skin a buck" and "plow a field all day long"—will make it out alive.

Loretta Lynn could do without Hank Jr.'s doomsaying, but as she sings in "You're Lookin' at Country" (1971), "this country girl would walk a country mile / To find her a good ole slow-talking country boy." Then, so as to underline her preference, she repeats, "I said a country boy." Not just any country boy will do. Drawl aside, Loretta makes plain she wants a workhorse with a worn shovel who, in exchange for a tour around the farm, will "show me a wedding band."

It's doubtful Lynn's narrator would have gone for the type Johnny Cash sings about on his first album, *Johnny Cash with His Hot and Blue Guitar!*—not that Cash's country boy would care. He has "no ills," "no bills," "no shoes," "no blues." A country boy's greatest privilege, Cash's "Country Boy" (1957) suggests, is his ignorance of the finer things. In part, he's happy with his "shaggy dog," fried fish, and "morning dew" because he hasn't been privy to much else.

Having little, Cash says, country boys have "a lot to lose." Cash, who by this stage in his life had traded Arkansas fields for a Memphis recording studio, spends a lot of time wishing he could get back to being a country boy, but his hot-and-blue guitar says otherwise. The truth is you couldn't go back if you wanted to, but would you go back even if you could?

It's when country boys leave the country, or are made aware of other lifestyles, that problems arise. They get nostalgic (Cash) or defensive (Hank Jr.), or they come down, in the case of Glen Campbell's "Country Boy (You Got Your Feet in L.A.)" (1975), with a bad case of impostor syndrome.

In the first song on his album *Rhinestone Cowboy*, Campbell sings about a country boy who has hit the big time:

You get a house in the hills
You're payin' everyone's bills
And they tell you that you're gonna go far
But in the back of my mind
I hear it time after time
Is that who you really are?

Having lived for so long on so much less—"I can remember the time," he sings, "When I sang my songs for free"—this country boy can't enjoy his change of fortune. His modest beginnings are both a grace and a liability. On the one hand, they keep him from getting carried away. On the other, they prevent him from being fully present. To do so, he fears, would be a self-betrayal. In the end, he realizes that he's going to have to choose. A country boy in Hollywood won't stay so for long.

What about a country boy in finance? In the video for Ricky Skaggs's 1985 hit "Country Boy," the bluegrass legend Bill Monroe accuses Skaggs of losing his bearings. The scene takes place in a Manhattan office building, where Skaggs sits behind a big desk in a business suit. Buzzed in by Skaggs's secretary, Monroe looks around. "I heard it was bad, boy, but I didn't know you'd sink to this," he says, at which point Skaggs whips out his guitar and tries to prove him wrong.

Monroe's disapproving presence turns Skaggs's foot stomper into a précis of Nashville's shifting sensibilities in the eighties. Skaggs had come up under Monroe's tutelage. He first played mandolin with Monroe's band when he was six years old. In his teens and twenties he had toured with the Stanley Brothers and the Country Gentlemen, more bluegrass royalty. With his high-lonesome voice and confident grasp of the bluegrass canon, Skaggs had often been regarded as the future of the genre, which is to say a faithful steward of its past. Now he was making mainstream country. Had he sold out?

You can take the boy out of the country but not the country out of the boy—that's what Skaggs contends. Despite ills and bills and all the rest of it, not to mention a streak of no. 1 records, a country boy is a country boy once and for all. He might work in a bank instead of a coal mine and live in a walk-up instead of a cabin in the woods, but deep down, he's still "a cotton picker," still "a hog caller chewing cud on the stile." Monroe isn't convinced. He shakes his head in disgust. "I'm just a country boy," Skaggs counters, over and over, "country boy at heart."

"Just a country boy." For Skaggs, the words are a pledge of allegiance. For Don Williams, however, they're a convenient excuse. In "I'm Just a Country Boy," a song first recorded by Harry Belafonte and that Williams took to no. 1 on the country charts in 1977, the meagerness wrapped up in the word "just" has real-world consequences.

Williams's country boy won't be marrying the woman he loves because he can't afford her. He can't afford much of anything. He might have, as the chorus says, "silver in the stars" and "gold in the morning sun," but they don't take sunshine at the jeweler's. And yet the "justness" of being a country boy resigns him to his letdown. The song is less a dirge than a shoulder shrug. "I'm just a country boy," Williams sings, as if to say, What did you expect?

Even so, resignation has its own complexity. That's the theme of another Williams song, the somber "Good Ole Boys like Me" (1979), which might as well be called "I'm Still Just a Country Boy." In that song, written by Bob McDill, the narrator looks back on a childhood full of sensually overwhelming contradictions and tries to reckon with his place in the world. In a chapter about Nashville from his travelogue *A Turn in the South*, V. S. Naipaul describes McDill's achievement as a kind of magic composed of "the calling up and recognition of impulses that on the surface were simple, but which, put together with music, made rich with a chorus, seemed to catch undefined places in the heart and memory."

The narrator of "Good Ole Boys like Me" recalls his gin-drunk father reading him the Bible at bedtime, lecturing him "about honor and things I should know," then staggering "a little as he went out the door." In the chorus, he declares his allegiance to Hank and Tennessee Williams, one a honky-tonk hero who forever exploded the boundaries of country music, the other a playwriting shake-scene who left Mississippi for New York and European cities and never stopped writing about displaced country people.

The country boy remembers falling asleep to the sounds of John R., a Nashville DJ who played rhythm and blues, and to the words of Thomas Wolfe "whispering in my head." Wolfe's two most famous novels, the autobiographical *Look Homeward, Angel* and the equally autobiographical *You Can't Go Home Again*, tell the story of a country boy's struggle to leave and return to the South. Don Williams's country boy has taken Wolfe's cue.

Unsettled by the death of a friend from substance abuse and, we might infer, by the fear of becoming a sentimental drunk like his old man, the country boy has "hit the road," and in more ways than one. He admits, in the final verse, that he has purposefully moderated his southern accent to sound like "the man on the six o'clock news." Maybe he's not a country boy at all. Maybe he never was one to begin with. "I was smarter than most," he says, "and I could choose."

Still, that he can recall these experiences and artifacts with such precision reveals how inured to them he remains. So much so that in the end, his statement about freedom of choice has been allayed by a kind of fatalism. "I guess," he concludes, "we're all gonna be what we're gonna be / So what do you do with good ole boys like me?"

I'm not sure how to take that question. Which way is it aimed? Is the "you" a world that no longer has much use for country boys? Or is the "you" the country boys who couldn't care less about their own relevance and so regard this narrator with suspicion? Don Williams's country boy is some combination of Skaggs's and Hank Jr.'s varieties. He's survived, all right, but in spite of his upbringing, not because of it, and what would it mean if in the end it turned out he wasn't a country boy, not even at heart?

"Good Ole Boys Like Me" has always reminded me of a painting by Marc Chagall called *I and the Village*, a framed poster of which hung on a wall in my Tennessee elementary school. Chagall completed *I and the Village* when he was in his midtwenties. He had traveled from Belarus to Paris and back. The painting, a spectacular of rapt disorientation, describes the churn.

In it, scenes from Vitsyebsk, the town where Chagall grew up, wheel around a polychromatic dreamscape. The characters are earthy, low down, and yet the picture radiates a kind of weightlessness. A man with a green face and white eyes holds a little tree of life. There's a woman milking a goat on a cow's cheek. In the background, a woman in blue skirts stands on her head, a kind of yin to the yang of a peasant shouldering a scythe.

I and the Village projects a cockeyed vision of village life. Later, Chagall would write in his memoir, *My Life*, that the flying figures and transmogrifying vistas that characterized his early breakthroughs had come in response to a desire, expressed in desperate prayers while walking the streets of Paris, to "see a new world."

In the third or fourth grade, I would not have had the vocabulary to articulate such thoughts, but I think I sensed, as I walked by *I and the Village* en route to class or hovered in front of it while waiting in line to go to the gym or restroom, something of Chagall's fraught relationship with his roots.

There was adoration in the Chagall, and there was also revulsion, nearness and distance, the red and the green. The artist loved this place and these people, even though, as I suspected, he wasn't one of them. His village wasn't Vitsyebsk; his village was the canvas. Likewise, Don Williams's "good ole boy," out of place in the country and the city alike, finds comfort, if nowhere else, in the country song, which for all its parochialism never comes off as provincial.

It's telling, if not surprising, that the chorus of "Good Ole Boys Like Me" commends, out of all the country singers in the canon, Hank Williams Sr., Hank Jr.'s dad. Ol' Hank, to my knowledge, didn't write any songs called "Country Boy." What he did write, unforgettably, was "Ramblin' Man" (1953), a minor-key manifesto, delivered in a brazen blue yodel, about the allure of the open road, a place he calls in another song "the lost highway."

What is a rambling man? A country boy gone rogue. As much as he sees the good in a simple, even simplistic way of life, a rambling man values his freedom more. He's a flight risk. In love and work, he's liable to unlatch at any moment, not caring who he works up or lets down in the process. Ashley Monroe, a country singer who has taken up the rambler mantle, describes the calculus in her song "I'm Good at Leavin'" (2015):

A couple times I said I do
A couple times I said we're through
I never really seem to get what I was needing
I'm good at packing up my car
I'm good at honky-tonks and bars

Waylon Jennings, in his 1974 cover of Ray Pennington's Hank-inspired "I'm a Ramblin' Man," puts it more bluntly: "You'd better move away / You're standin' too close to the flame."

More than a personal liability, though, Hank's rambling man is also something of a jongleur. Hank recorded "Ramblin' Man" under the auspices of his alter ego, Luke the Drifter. The songs Hank recorded as Luke tend to deliver morality tales. Luke is a kind of itinerant preacher, a wandering prophet whose home church seems to consist solely of Hank Williams, whose own songs, reflective of his life, were often about carousing, heavy drinking, and existential despair.

Instead of Dr. Jekyll to the country boy's Mr. Hyde, Hank's rambling man is a wiser, more bruised iteration of himself. He seems older than Hank, at once more frightening and more reasonable, cut off from society, and yet drawing from a deeper source. He hasn't abdicated responsibility so much as secured the necessary distance to appraise experience and report back. Rambling, in this sense, is the process by which a country boy grows up.

"Ramblin' Man" was never released as a single. The song was the B side to "Take These Chains from My Heart," a honky-tonk ballad that went to no. 1 following Hank's death, at age twenty-nine, on New Year's Day 1953. Hank's passing translated "Ramblin' Man" into a last will and testament. "And when I'm gone," he sings,

and at my grave you stand
Just say God's called home your ramblin' man

Like John Denver, Ol' Hank invokes the Almighty. "Let me travel this land," he prays,

from the mountains to the sea
'Cause that's the life I believe He meant for me

One thanks his stars he's a country boy. The other thanks his he isn't only that. The question is not whether or not to be a country boy. The question is, What kind of country boy are you going to be?

THE WHINE

The first song I ever loved was "On the Other Hand," by Randy Travis. It was the first single from Travis's debut album, *Storms of Life*—and it was the third single too. The song fizzled when Travis first released it in the summer of 1985, so he rereleased it the following spring, figuring it might fare better after "1982," the album's second single, entered the top 10.

This time, "On the Other Hand" went to no. 1 on the charts. It was on country radio all the time, and because my mother listened to country radio all the time, I learned the song, as I'd learned countless others, through osmosis. We lived in Davidson County, in the hills due north of Nashville, a place where country music was less a form of entertainment than an atmospheric feature, as ubiquitous as clouds and often as nebulous.

"On the Other Hand" was different. Travis's deep nasal whine, a mix of range and grog and woebegone, blew through the blur. His voice seemed to summon Hank Williams by way of a bullfrog. He was, among other things, an irresistible parody. I stood in front of the fireplace in the living room. I pinched my nostrils. "On one hand, I count the reasons I could stay with you," I started, pausing to release my nose hold and inhale again before continuing, "And hold you close to me, all night long."

The song finds Travis weighing the pros and cons of continuing an affair. In the pros column is the pleasure his mistress provides. "And on that hand," Travis sings, "I see no reason why it's wrong." "But on the other hand," he continues, "there's a golden band." If, in the end, Travis is leaning toward calling off the fling, the song is hardly a defense of fidelity. Travis's divided heart is still with his lover, whom he credits with reviving his joie de vivre. "I've got to hand it to you girl," he tells her in the final verse, "you're something else."

Storms of Life went on to sell more than three million copies and win the 1986 Academy of Country Music award for Album of the Year. It has about it a kind of creaky coherence. The songs are about cheating, leaving, and crisis. The album begins with "On the Other Hand" and ends with "There'll Always Be a Honky Tonk Somewhere"—the messy bedroom leads inevitably to the barstool, with trips along the way to memory lane ("Digging Up Bones," "1982"), the confessional ("Reasons I Cheat"), the railroad crossing ("Send My Body"), and the therapist ("Messin' With My Mind").

Thematically, the songs don't buck tradition so much as begrudgingly capitulate to it. In "No Place like Home," the single released after "On the Other Hand," the wholesome truth of the titular cliché dawns on the narrator with the force of revelation—but only after his wife has sent him packing. In the end, the song isn't about home; it's about the nostalgia that swirls in the wake of wrecking it.

The gulf between my interest and Travis's intentions must have given my parents a rise. They marveled at how I knew every word. And I did know every word—or at least knew how to sing them, if not quite what they were saying. What little I could gather, which may have been only a vague notion of friction between the sexes, felt odd and slightly frightening.

Indeed, country songs were not unlike horror films. Both derived power from the ridiculous. Both dealt in extremes, in worst-case scenarios. Both played out, in large part, under cover of dark. There were differences, of course. Instead of monsters, country songs featured carousers. Instead of curses, the toughest luck. Still, one seemed as outré as the other. In childhood, masked murderers and bill collectors are comparably remote.

There was a sense, however, in which the lyrics were beside the point, for in the end, as in the beginning, what I loved first and foremost about Randy Travis was his voice. It was the whine that resonated, that wavering, wind-burred bellow, the sadness and the apathy of it, the pathetic beauty. I wondered how in the world he'd gotten away with making such a noise.

Of all the wisdom my parents imparted—to say *sir*, to say *ma'am*, to hold doors for the people behind you, to shake with a firm hand, and so on—the bit they were most emphatic about was whining. Nobody, they said, respected a whiner. It was wrong for the living to want to die, and that's what whining communicated: I'd rather be dead.

Tied to the warning about whining was a second commandment: thou shalt not mope. Whining had to do with talk. Moping had to with posture, with physical crestfallenness, lethargy exaggerated for effect. Put them together and you'd get a loser sulking about with a moan on his lips, which, to hear my parents tell it, was a terrible look. And yet there was Randy Travis, whining without apology, loafing in music videos, and singing on the radio in a tone of voice for which I would have been sent off to my room.

Travis's whine, truth be told, didn't sound all that sorry to me. It had integrity. It was possessed of the languor of late summer. It felt of a piece with the North Nashville landscape. In a place where the Ford Broncos and tobacco barns had seen better days, where wasps and poison ivy reigned tyrannically, where trees sagged under the weight of bug-gored fruit, and tick-eared beagle hounds panted in the hot shade, how else, I wondered, should singing sound?

His was foothill music—not the soaring anthems of mountaintops, not the sober hymns of the horizontal plains, but a tremulous waver between the two, between the lower tiers of heaven and the higher rungs of hell, between delight and dejection, among hesitancy, agony, and force of will. There was loss in it—not the pain of loss per se, but the shame that comes from knowing you were right to have lost, and that if things stayed the same, you were probably going to lose a lot more.

Travis was twenty-seven when *Storms of Life* came out. As a teenager in North Carolina, he'd dropped out of high school and done a bid in county jail for car theft. Singing was an escape that reified the need to. His world-sick timbre was the bruised fruit of nonchalance chastened by disgrace. Travis's whine was audible, and yet it retained an urgent, under-the-breath intimacy. It was as if a hostile hand was pressed up hard against that hole in the heart where feeling comes from. Even muffled, though, Travis's sound was trenchant, cutting. It was the outermost echo of a buried cry.

That "On the Other Hand" sounded fresh, newfangled even, in the mideighties highlighted just how gassy Nashville country had become. Critics tagged Travis a neotraditionalist. But there was nothing *neo* about him. He sounded less like a fusion of contemporary and classic country than the rearrival of a sound that had never not been around. The final song on *Storms of Life*, "There'll Always Be a Honky Tonk Somewhere," opens around the album like a crowded room, at once turning the collection into an homage to honky-tonk music and an essay about the indispensability, in a weary world, of the whine.

You can take the singer out of the doldrums, but not the doldrums out of the singer. Even as Travis became one of Nashville's most reliable song dogs, charting single after hit single and selling millions of records, he kept whining and moping and moaning, perhaps nowhere more feelingly than on the 1990 single "He Walked on Water." Over a harmonica and the spare plucking of an acoustic guitar, Travis relays pithy anecdotes about his great-grandfather. The man is ancient. He has one foot in the present and one in another century. "He said he'd been a cowboy," Travis sings,

> when he was young
> And he could handle a rope and he was good with a gun

The man's age, know-how, and eccentricity ("He wore," Travis sings, "starched white shirts buttoned at the neck") had cast a spell over the young Travis. In at least two ways, the great-grandfather is like a god. One: the span of his years is unfathomable. Two: the love he engenders borders on worship, hence the one-line chorus—"I thought that he walked on water."

I knew right away what Travis was getting at. Once or twice a year, my own great-grandfather on my mother's father's side would drive down from West Virginia to visit us. His name was Enos, a name lifted from the first chapters of the book of Genesis, and he seemed to be as old as Genesis, as mysterious. He was a mountain man. He had worked as a coal miner. His right hand had been shattered in an accident, and one of the fingers had reset at a ninety-degree angle. When you shook it, the cocked finger pressed into your palm, a sensation that simultaneously bridged and ossified the distance between you.

He spent the days shooting squirrels in the woods around the house. If not "good with a gun," as Travis's great-grandfather is in the song, he was loose with the trigger. We'd hear bullets ripping through trees and ricocheting off the barn. At dusk, he'd walk over the hill and empty his field bag beneath the shade tree by the porch. "I looked at him and he looked at me," he told me once, holding a squirrel up by the tail, "and if I hadn't pulled the trigger first, he'd be the one sitting here gutting me."

I was struck in particular by the bridge in "He Walked on Water":

And he was ninety years old in sixty-three
And I loved him and he loved me
And lord, I cried the day he died

'Cause I thought that he walked on water

The lines decried something that, up until I heard them, I had not known that I knew: that my great-grandfather would not live forever and that this was true for everyone I loved.

"I thought," Travis sings. The verb is in the past tense. He doesn't think such thoughts anymore.

John Berger wrote that storytellers are secretaries who take their orders from Death. "The file," Berger writes, "is full of sheets of uniformly black paper but they have eyes for reading them and from this file they construct a story for the living." "He Walked On Water," like much of Travis's music, was made, I think, within the umbra of mortality. It wasn't I-want-to-die music; it was we're-all-going-to-die music. It was the soundtrack to a story for the living that also kept the dead alive.

Travis was inducted into the Country Music Hall of Fame in 2016. At the time, his reputation was recovering from a series of public mistakes and private misfortunes. He'd been arrested for drunk driving outside a Texas church. The booking photograph had made the rounds. In Johnny Cash's famous El Paso mugshot, taken after he was apprehended for smuggling pills across the Mexican border, he looks like Johnny Cash, nonplussed, righteously ambivalent. Travis, by comparison, looks disturbing. His eye is black, his nose is swollen. There is blood between his brows.

Shortly after the arrest, a video surfaced of Travis stumbling naked into a convenience store, drunkenly demanding cigarettes. Unlike Cash, whose music was inextricable from his person, Travis hadn't been a persona so much as a voice delivering songs. Now country's lethargic prophet was becoming a lightning rod.

Travis had suffered a stroke in 2013. There had been talk that he might never speak, let alone sing, again. But at the hall-of-fame ceremony, Travis took the microphone. Phalanxed by his wife and the singer Garth Brooks, who had removed his black cowboy hat in tribute, Travis made it through the first stanza of "Amazing Grace."

His voice was weak and inchoate. That he managed to get any words out at all was something of a triumph, and yet from somewhere deep inside the flickering shadow of the sound he used to make, you could hear it—the whine had survived. On the one hand, it said, "I'll keep going, but I don't have to like it." And on the other, "I'll sing the sorrow if the sorrow is all I have to sing."

TO BE AT HOME EVERYWHERE

What Novalis says about philosophy—that in reality it is a homesickness—is true also of country music, though philosophers and country singers have different ideas about what home is. In philosophy, home is a state of perfect understanding. Philosophers, Novalis writes, long to "be at home everywhere." But country singers long not so much for the outside world—or, for that matter, the world to come—but rather for the world as they once knew it, typically in childhood. The philosopher hopes for a home she's never seen, while the country singer mourns for the home she may never see again.

Of all the homesick country albums by all the homesick country singers, few explore homesickness more searchingly than Dolly Parton's *My Tennessee Mountain Home*. In eleven bittersweet songs, lasting a little more than thirty-three minutes total, Dolly revisits the fraught days after she first moved to Nashville, when the future was a stranger, the past a dear friend, and the present a disorienting swirl of memories and dreams.

The circumstances surrounding the making of *My Tennessee Mountain Home* are worth noting. The album was Dolly's eleventh solo release, and yet it was sort of a second debut. In the six years since the first, 1967's *Hello, I'm Dolly*, she had become best known not as a solo artist but as Porter Wagoner's duet partner and deferential sidekick on the popular syndicated TV program *The Porter Wagoner Show*.

The two were the oddest of showbiz couples. Porter was a lanky, dog-faced crooner. A fixture of country radio through the fifties and sixties, he was at his most compelling in front of a camera. He wore sequined suits, bolo ties, and a blonde pompadour. He had cornball charm and ductile made-for-TV expressions. His eyebrows, high and arching, had minds of their own.

With Dolly, who joined the show in 1967, Porter found an amiable foil. Her blonde wigs and bright dresses, every bit the match to Porter's farm boy glam, seemed less like cover for a lack of talent than the visible manifestation of an inner might. The tension between them was palpable. Alongside Dolly, Porter was like a kid with a crush: giddy, cartoonish, charmingly pathetic.

It made for good TV. The show, which at its peak reached more than three million viewers, still bore Porter's imprimatur, but Dolly was the star. Her vocals, delivered seamlessly through a quicksilver smile, were fit, all at once, for the corner bar, the choir loft, and Carnegie Hall. They turned everything they touched, Porter's midwestern deadpan included, into glitter.

By the early seventies, it was clear that Dolly would need to shed Porter if she wanted to ascend to the first ranks of country stardom and venture into mainstream pop. First, however, she needed confidence as well as the assurance that branching out didn't have to mean betraying her roots. James Baldwin once said that he had to finish *Go Tell It on the Mountain*, his autobiographical novel about growing up in the church, before he could write anything else. Likewise, *My Tennessee Mountain Home* is a tribute that doubles as an excision. It put Dolly in touch with her rootstock while also clearing the ground for her relaunch.

My Tennessee Mountain Home wasn't the first time Dolly had made music about her upbringing. "Back through the years I go wanderin' once again / Back to the seasons of my youth," begins "Coat of Many Colors," a hit single from 1971 about her mother's sewing and the severe blessings of growing up poor. But never before had her album-length projects been so focused. There's not a single love song on *Mountain Home*, not a sacred song, not a standard. The album cover features a Polaroid of the shack in the Smoky Mountains where Dolly was raised, and the songs open the door and step inside. Dolly sings about her mother's kitchen in "Old Black Kettle," her father's clothes in "Daddy's Working Boots," anxious nights and cold winters in "In the Good Old Days (When Times Were Bad)," her brothers and sisters in "The Better Part of Life," and even the country physician who delivered her in "Dr. Robert F. Thomas." The songs are sentimental, sometimes cloyingly so, but that's the point. *Mountain Home*, at heart, is a record about nostalgia and the human tendency to glorify what's already gone until we get a hold of the next good thing.

Dolly's wistful compositions are elevated by the descriptive power of her songwriting, which can make a marvel of even the most banal childhood episode. "Sitting on the front porch," the title track begins, "on a summer afternoon / In a straightback chair on two legs, leaned against the wall." The lyric is about nothing but sitting in a chair, and yet it's hard not to hear in the chair's slow tilt a faint whisper of the very leave-taking that, all these years later, has given rise to the song. The kid isn't content to sit in the chair the proper way. She's bored and a touch impertinent, so against the wishes of her parents, perhaps while they're not looking, she leans back on two legs. She's less grounded now, not flying but not idling either, even as she's still braced by the wall.

It's all there: past and future, dream world and real world, safety and risk. The lyric illustrates the dueling sentiments— the need to leave, the desire to stay—that Dolly lays out in the album's opening track, a dramatic reading of a letter she posted back to her parents once she got to Nashville. "I cried almost all the way," she says, "and I wanted to turn around a few times and come back, but you know how bad I've always wanted to go to Nashville and be a singer and songwriter, and I believe that if I try long enough and hard enough that someday, I'll make it."

Although these songs are full of praise for a simpler way

of living, there's nothing spare about their production. The album typifies the Nashville sound, a studio aesthetic built on a contradictory assumption, that country music—that is, music from a poor, rural, slightly rusty perspective—should be rendered flawlessly and with a polish.

Produced by Bob Ferguson at RCA Records, *Mountain Home* features a who's who of ace session players: Bobby Thompson on guitar, Johnny Gimble on fiddle, Pete Drake on pedal steel, the blind and brilliant Hargus "Pig" Robbins on piano. A lonesome harmonica moans. A harp frames everything in the mist of flashback. The nearly too good to be true sonics feel in keeping with the spirit of Dolly's project. Just as the homesick mind will turn a shack into a mansion, Ferguson turns Dolly's revelries into overwrought anthems. Throughout, her voice is warm and intimate but, like a campfire in a dry forest, liable at any moment to flare.

In isolation, these songs can seem mawkish, naive. Taken together, though, they form a tough-enough narrative. It goes something like this: Dolly leaves home ("With a suitcase in my hand and a hope in my heart"), Dolly misses home ("Remember all the fun we had / Back when they say times were bad"), and Dolly returns home ("We're all together once again / For the first time in I don't know when"), only to find that home isn't the same as when she left it ("[Mama] says it sure is lonesome now / Since all of us kids are all growed up and gone").

Mountain Home concludes with a barn burner called "Down on Music Row." On first listen, it feels a little misplaced. The subject isn't nostalgia but fortitude through disillusionment. In a series of humorous anecdotes, Dolly rehashes the hoops she had to go through to find a receptive audience for her songs. "They said that I could leave a tape," she writes of an encounter at a record label, "But they'd suggest I didn't wait / 'Cause everyone was awful busy / Down on Music Row."

From Waylon Jennings's "Are You Sure Hank Done It This Way" to Jason Aldean's "Crazy Town," there's a long and ever-expanding list of country songs about the rigmarole of the music business. What sets Dolly's entry apart is its mix of willful resignation and playfulness. The song evokes an old-timey hoedown. *Mountain Home*'s swooning sentimentalism has been shoved aside. Just as time has chastened Dolly's memories of her childhood home, the years have also tempered her desire to make it in Nashville on Nashville's terms. "Down on Music Row / Down on Music Row," she sings in the chorus, belting the words as if simulating an audition, before toning it down to deliver the finger wag: "If you want to be a star / That's where you've got to go."

She sounds liberated. It's as if here, at the end of the album, her homesickness having been flagged not merely as a powerful feeling but also as a shorthand for the human condition, she has finally slipped out of homesickness's hold.

Dolly would quit *The Porter Wagoner Show* in 1974. She would immortalize the split in "I Will Always Love You," the second single from her first bona fide post-Porter release, *Jolene*. A few years after that, in a prime-time interview done in the midst of a stadium tour, she would tell Barbara Walters, "I want to be able to walk into any place and [hear people] say, There's Dolly." She's sitting on a tour bus when she says these words, but you get the sense she's still that girl on the porch, leaning her chair back against the wall and longing, like a philosopher, to be at home everywhere.

UNLIKELY LULLABIES

During the colicky first weeks following the birth of our son, Beckett, my wife and I would take turns rising in the night to rock the little bugger back to sleep. Without recourse to breast milk or the pacifying whispers Emily floated into his burning little ears, I often resorted to dancing him around the living room of our termite-infested rental on Capitol Hill, all the while singing whatever lyrics I could call to mind.

For whatever reason, the one song that presented itself wholesale was "I'm No Stranger to the Rain," the cantering Sonny Curtis number that Keith Whitley took to the top of the country music charts in 1989. More *Divine Comedy* than "Frere Jacques," "I'm No Stranger" is hardly a lullaby. The verses map one maverick's trek through heartache, high water, and hellfire. "I fought with the devil," Whitley sings, "Got down on his level, / But I never gave in, so he gave up on me."

The Dantean undertones are amplified, in Whitley's version, by the singer's personal misadventures. When "I'm No Stranger" was released, it looked as if Whitley might just become the biggest country music star in the world. The song was his third no. 1 in a row off *Don't Close Your Eyes*, an album that seamlessly welded old and nouveau Nashville sounds, steel guitar and saxophone, Merle Haggard lilt and Lionel Richie suavity, cowboy boots and beardstache.

On a Tuesday morning, four months after "I'm No Stranger" hit the radio, Whitley's brother-in-law found him unconscious in his house in North Nashville. At Baptist Hospital downtown, Whitley was pronounced dead. The cause was alcohol poisoning. News reports said that he had consumed the equivalent of twenty shots of 100-proof whiskey. He was thirty-four years old.

Night after humid night, unable to summon an innocuous cradle song, I wrangled my voice into Whitley's smeared baritone, looked into Beckett's tear-swamped eyes, and began:

I'm no stranger to the rain
I'm a friend of thunder
Friend, is it any wonder
Lightning strikes me?

That I remembered the words was a shock. Although I grew up a couple of miles from the house where Whitley drank himself to death, and my brother had played on baseball teams with his son, Jesse, it had been decades since I had heard "I'm No Stranger to the Rain."

Perhaps the reshuffling of the song to the top of my mental playlist was a fluke. Perhaps any old berceuse would have flown. But there is something in me that wants to believe in a living music, in a melody that advances and prevails on us at formative moments, corralling our chaos, if only for the space of three-and-a-half minutes, into the simple, liberating stockade of verse, chorus, verse.

"You have to grow up, start paying the rent and have your heart broken, before you can understand country," Emmylou Harris once said. The truth was that Beckett had been born amid a fit of trials and disenchantments not out of keeping with the litany set out in the song. Shortly after our wedding, Emily and I had moved from Washington to Wichita to begin editing a flailing city magazine. We had delusions of grandeur. We envisioned a *New Yorker* for the Midwest. The poet Albert Goldbarth lived in Wichita. The novelist Antonya Nelson had grown up there. *National Geographic* photographer Jim Richardson had a studio in nearby Lindsborg. The local newspaper had recently laid off a beloved political cartoonist.

If we could rope the right contributors into the mix, we felt we could generate excitement, win some awards, maybe even start a movement. Everywhere we heard the whispers of untold stories. How many *In Cold Bloods* were waiting to be uncovered? How many investigative pieces about Koch Industries or Boeing, two major companies with local headquarters? How many reappraisals of "Wichita Lineman," "Wichita Vortex Sutra," *The Wizard of Oz*?

It was perhaps the best chance we'd ever have to create something meaningful. I was twenty-five. Emily was twenty-four. We'd gone to journalism school. We'd worked under the hood of magazines in DC. Now, at last, we were behind the wheel.

Then the economy crashed, clients withdrew ads, readers canceled subscriptions, and the publisher, who had been enthusiastic about our vision, or had at least pretended to be, decided to shutter the magazine. Eight months after landing in Kansas, we said goodbye to Kansas, having lost our confidence and all our savings. Back in Washington, we moved in with Emily's mother. We were fortunate, but we were feeling like failures. You assume a certain continuity of experience before and after exchanging vows, but in less than a year's time, the ground beneath us had shifted dramatically, perhaps irrevocably, and we weren't sure what we were going to do.

We submitted a hundred resumes, met contacts for coffee, submitted a hundred more. Emily took an internship in the city. I took a job editing online textbooks. It was work, and we were happy to have it, even if the situation wasn't workable long term. We were still catching our breath when we learned that Emily was pregnant. The news kicked everything into a high gear. We scraped together two-months' rent and signed a one-year lease on a place on Capitol Hill. Nine months later, feeling nine years older, we hauled Beckett through the front door.

Backlit by these anxieties, "I'm No Stranger" proved a prescient lullaby. Here was a song a father could sing his son without feeling like he was lying. The lyrics had—have—verisimilitude. The bridge, in particular, is a frank admission of human frailty. "But it's hard to keep believing / I'll even come out even / While the rain beats a hole in the ground," our troubadour confesses, before disclosing, so as to add immediacy to the forecast, "And tonight it's really coming down."

For all its straight shooting, the lingering tone of "I'm No Stranger" is bullish. Rough handles, after all, produce calloused hands. The rain-soaked narrator has become an ace at auguring the weather and has learned, consequently, how to hunker down. "But I'll put the clouds behind me," he goes on. "That's how the Man designed me / To ride the wind and dance in a hurricane."

Dancing in a hurricane. A startling image, it's also the least believable line in the song. Up to that point, "I'm No Stranger" unspools like a countrypolitan revamp of "Man of Constant Sorrow," the folk ballad popularized by Ralph Stanley, in whose band Whitley, at age sixteen, along with childhood friend Rickie Skaggs, had cut his chops. Sure, there's a touch of triumphalism in the lyrics ("But through it all I withstood the pain"), but no revelry, no gloating. This makes the detour into "Singin' in the Rain" schmaltz all the more unpalatable. Whitley, for his part, seems to concede as much; his voice peters out at this point on a belch of a bass note.

Dancing, we suspect, is the last thing this narrator would do. He'd pull on his cigarette, curse a bit under his breath. He might stomp the floor with his boots, kick up some dust, but never heel-toe do-si-do, not after the season he's lived through. There's a difference between being undeterred by darkness and being a dumbass.

Then again, dancing was the last thing I expected to be doing either, and yet there I was, stuck in those hurricane hours of early fatherhood, dead tired, drowning a little, and doing just that. What song and dance, I wondered, had I been swept up into? Was this a *danse macabre*, that medieval allegory that fashioned life as a great swaying together toward the grave?

In paintings and lithographs, Death, typically represented

by a skeleton, unites the hands of kings and beggars alike. Strangers, even sworn enemies, become partners by virtue of their shared destination. There's that scene at the end of Ingmar Bergman's *Seventh Seal* where a traveling actor has a vision of Death leading a knight, a blacksmith, a flirt, and a widow over the hillside. "They dance away from the dawn," the actor—his name is Jof—tells his wife, "and it's a solemn dance toward the dark lands, while the rain washes their faces and cleans the salt of the tears from their cheeks."

In the scene, Death almost seems like a savior. "I'll close your eyes so you can't see," Ralph Stanley sings in his haunting classic "O Death,"

> This very hour come and go with me
> Death I come to take the soul
> Leave the body and leave it cold

But Bergman's grim reaper takes the body, too. So far as we know, none of the figures in his parade have contracted the plague, which has decimated the countryside across which they've journeyed. Nevertheless, the slow parade is noteworthy for who isn't included—Jof and his wife, who happen to be new parents.

Beckett and I were partners all right—even before we left the delivery room, I had pledged myself forever—but our harried bounces and turns about the house were far more of a practical solution (and a pathetic one at that) than the stuff of allegory and art house film.

We had been brought together by colic, not by death, which is to say, we had been brought together by life. Judging by the volume and intensity of Beckett's cries and my inability to ease his pain for any length of time, death seemed at times as if it might have been preferable. Beckett's face, so handsome when calm, balled up like a fist in the heat of his fits. He weighed ten, maybe fifteen pounds, but his shrieks were gun blasts ricocheting off the walls. Like a bull, he heaved and shook, threw his body forward and jerked back, and I tried my best, a rodeo cowboy if not a rodeo clown, to hang on.

A catch-all term for various stomach issues in newborns, colic has no medical cure. There is no medicine you can administer, no shortcut you can take. Everybody has a solution, which they posit in the form of questions: Have you tried putting a hot cloth on the baby's stomach? Are you swaddling him snugly enough? When is the last time you gave him a warm bath? In the end, you're left on your own to find temporary cathartics until the child outgrows the pain.

Even so, I was hell-bent on getting Beckett to quit screaming before he woke up the upstairs neighbors, who, for all I knew, might well raise the issue with the landlord. I was equally bent on getting back to bed myself. How many days can you operate on little-to-no sleep before your boss takes notice?

I lived for the moment when the wailing and contorting gave way to a sighing and slumping into calm, but when that moment did come, and sometimes for quite a while afterward, I went on singing, not wanting to break whatever spell had been cast, and then the whole thing seemed to morph into something else entirely.

Keith Whitley died young, but I think he was older than his years. I heard a recording once of him singing "Mountain Dew" with Ralph Stanley in the 1960s. He couldn't have been more than seventeen at the time. Already he sounded as if he'd lived hard and fast and crashed and come back a bit contrite and equally recalcitrant. It could be that he was only pretending, singing confidently about things he'd only heard about in songs. It could be that songs, the closer they get to the bone, are as good an education as anything.

I had never felt urgency like the urgency I felt in fatherhood. Even in the first days of Beckett's life, I wanted to transfer to him everything I'd learned and experienced. I wanted to keep him from being blindsided by life as I had been, but I didn't know where or when or how to start.

What I did know was a song about rain, and as I sang it in hopes of quieting Beckett's screaming, I felt the screams and anxieties in my own head opening, clearing. A kind of grace had come floating back unbidden to dance me through the hurricane.

THE LAST COWBOY SONG

In *The Searchers*, a photograph from David Levinthal's 2015 series, *History*, a cowboy in a high-crowned hat stands on a ridge watching the sun go down. The sky and the desert landscape fuse and flare in the distance. The cowboy, his back to the camera, hip cocked, rifle resting on his shoulder, looks simultaneously spent and imperious, at once a bemused sheriff and an escaped outlaw. As the title of the picture indicates, the cowboy in question is Ethan Edwards, the ornery rebel played by an indignant John Wayne in John Ford's 1956 vigilante Western, *The Searchers*. But the figure in the photograph isn't really Edwards either. A closer look reveals him to be neither a cowboy nor a Hollywood leading man pretending to be a cowboy but rather a plastic figurine of an actor playing the part.

Levinthal's photograph, in other words, isn't really about *The Searchers*. Although the toy is meticulously outfitted after Wayne's character in the early minutes of the movie (red button-down shirt, high-waisted jeans cuffed at the bottom, holstered pistol hanging off the hip), and its rectilinear stance signals Wayne, an actor for whom standing still was high drama, you won't find this particular moment in the film. Sure, it's the kind of scene that *could* have been in the film. Levinthal's diorama convincingly evokes Monument Valley, that intransigent stretch of Arizona desert where a gaggle of Texas rangers trail the formidable Comanche warrior who has murdered Edwards's brother and sister-in-law and kidnapped his niece (Natalie Wood). Indeed, it's a scene you're almost certain *must* have been in the film, but one that, alas, does not exist.

Instead, the photograph depicts a valediction that the film makes possible. It describes the afterlife of images in the imaginations of impressionable kids who, by way of plastic toys scattered across bedroom floors, *become* their Hollywood heroes for a moment that lasts forever. Inflating the figurine in the foreground to near-human scale, Levinthal, who was born in San Francisco in 1949, exalts childhood fantasy while at the same time reducing the American frontier, as glorified by Hollywood Westerns of the forties and fifties, to the stuff of toy boxes and playgrounds. "My subject," Levinthal once said, "is a West that never was but always will be."

Recently, I found myself in mind of *The Searchers* when my daughter Rosie asked, from the backseat of the Pilot, whether instead of NPR, we could listen to "those old cowboy songs." I knew what she meant. In the glove compartment, crammed among Jiffy Lube receipts, ice scrapers, trash, and various paperwork, I keep a scuffed yet stealthy CD copy of Marty Robbins's 1959 album *Gunfighter Ballads and Trail Songs*—a Western set to music if Nashville ever produced one.

Like Outkast's *ATLiens* (1996) and Arcade Fire's *Funeral* (2004), *Gunfighter Ballads* is a near-perfect album to listen to while driving. This has to do with the music, which evokes swift movement across great distances, and it has to do with Marty Robbins, who, in addition to being a popular Golden Age country singer, raced stock cars professionally, sometimes running a purple-and-yellow Dodge Charger, sometimes a Plymouth Belvedere with the number 777 on the door. In a NASCAR career that included some thirty-five races, Robbins finished in the top 10 six times. His yellow track suit is behind glass at the Ryman Auditorium, where Robbins, who died from a heart attack in 1982, regularly performed as a cast member at the Grand Ole Opry.

One of my father's good friends, a forklift salesman with checker-flag dreams, used to hang out in the infield of the racetrack at the Nashville fairgrounds. He told me a story about how Robbins was once winning a race with ten laps left to go when, to the surprise of his crew and the crowd alike, he veered off the track. People went running. "What's wrong, Marty?" they said. "Is the engine on fire? Is it going to blow?" Robbins took off his helmet and climbed out of the cabin. "No," he said. "I've got to go on at the Opry in about fifteen minutes, and I don't want to be late."

Racing is about sustained focus. What looks like recklessness is really negotiated restraint. The way to keep moving is to never stop holding back until you let go. It takes muscle and dash, a heavy foot and a flicking wrist. The impossible combo figures prominently in *Hell on Wheels*, a B-movie from 1967, in which Robbins, forty-two at the time, plays a car-racing country singer whose jealous brother, hoping to challenge Robbins for the checkered flag, falls in with a local toughie who happens to be running a moonshine racket.

In the final scenes, the film devolves into a high-speed shootout on winding Tennessee back roads. Windshields shatter. Tires kick up loose gravel. Robbins's brother takes a bullet in the side. Heading into a sharp curve by a pond, Robbins lays off the gas and steers into the slide before gunning it again when the road straightens out. The moonshine king is reckless, all power and no grace. He hits the curve at full bore, and the curve hits back. Rolling into the water, his car erupts in flames. The film concludes with Robbins singing a cautionary ditty to his niece: "So don't fly too high in the sky butterfly / If you fly very high in the sky you'll find the sun may burn your wings."

Do I drive faster when I'm listening to Marty Robbins, or does it only feel that way? Speed, in any case, is an essential aspect of *Gunfighter Ballads*. The album, Robbins's fourth and most enduring (the Library of Congress added it to the National Recording Registry in 2017), was recorded in a single day at Bradley's Film and Recording Studio, on the stretch of Nashville's Sixteenth Avenue South that would become known as Music Row. The twelve tracks blow by in a little over thirty-five minutes. They come at you one right after the other, and yet they feel neither dashed off nor prematurely halted, but rather like the efficient and sometimes giddy expressions of an elusive love.

Instead of a figurine of a famous Hollywood cowboy, the cover of *Gunfighter Ballads* features Robbins in costume. Dressed in black from hat to boot heel, he is crouched down, ready. His right hand is on his six-shooter. He's a split second from drawing, from firing. Pow.

Robbins was born in Glendale, Arizona, in 1925. His grandfather, a former Texas Ranger with a Wild Bill mustache, gave him firsthand accounts of cattle drives and train robberies. As with Levinthal, Westerns were an orienting influence. Robbins's leading man, however, wasn't John Wayne but Gene Autry, the Singing Cowboy. Per the conventions of the genre, Autry's black-and-white pictures, which lit up the screens of southwestern cinemas before World War II, were full of outlaws, horses, saloons, and shootouts. The difference was that, in an Autry Western, songs had agency.

Autry's ballads often delivered lessons about working hard ("Back in the Saddle Again") and doing good ("Have I Told You Lately That I Love You"), but the real moral of any Autry Western was that all could be forgiven so long as you could fashion it into a handsome melody. In the middle of a stickup on a dusty street, Autry would start playing his guitar, often while still riding his horse, and the pistol wielders, hell-bent on bloodshed only a moment earlier, would be so taken with his singing, which reflected something of their own experience, that they'd lower their rifles and break into applause.

Robbins's voice bore Autry's imprimatur. His velvety baritone, better suited for brass than banjos, combined regal crooning with a touch of lachrymosity. One Texas DJ took to calling him "the boy with a teardrop in his voice." Physically, though, Robbins projected a lively toughness. His face was flinty, visorlike. "You've got eyes," June Carter joked with him once at the Opry, "like two deep blue pools of water, with a diving board right between them." The sea winds in the Solomon Islands, where Robbins had served as a navy coxswain during the war, had sculpted his cheeks and jowls into their own shield.

Robbins was a gas on stage. Between verses in live performances, he was always toying with the crowd, always winking and rolling his eyes. Was he bored by the sound of his own voice? Quite the opposite: he was amused by it. It was as if he knew he had gotten away with something. His onstage gestures, sometimes endearing, sometimes distracting, were attempts to bring the audience into complicity. "I'm in this business," he told one interviewer, "because I despise honest labor."

Robbins's first records for Columbia were feints in several possible directions. On his debut album, *Rock'n Roll'n Robbins* (1956), he covered Little Richard's "Long Tall Sally," Chuck Berry's "Maybellene," and Hank Williams's "Long Gone Lonesome Blues." The breakthrough came with 1958's *Marty Robbins*, a slick collection of doo-wop and whistle pop-country chestnuts about teenage lust and letdown. Arranged by Ray Conniff, who had worked with Johnny Mathis and Rosemary Clooney, the single "A White Sport Coat (and a Pink Carnation)" sold a million copies. With its concise evocation of pre-prom awkwardness, the song rose to number two on the *Billboard* pop charts and became a staple of high school dances.

Robbins could make passable music in any number of genres, fashioning himself as a bebopper, a blues singer, or a country crooner, but in each case he sounded derivative, noncommittal. His covers of Hank Williams weren't sufficiently wretched, his rockabilly numbers were too sedate, and his stint as a teen heartthrob was impracticable. He was already in his midthirties.

Gunfighter Ballads was hardly a predictable pivot. Then again, it didn't emerge ex nihilo. Two years before the album was released, Robbins had played a mercenary in a minor Western called *Raiders of Old California* (1957). Shortly thereafter, he penned a one-off title song for *The Hanging*

Tree (1959), a film about greedy Montana gold diggers starring Gary Cooper and Maria Schell. But what was surprising about *Gunfighter Ballads* was just how totally the teenybopper became the troubadour. The songs were removed enough from Robbins's life experience to liberate him from the pretense of authenticity, yet near enough to his heart to call forth his best instincts. From the first song, the hard-charging "Big Iron," Robbins's need for speed and concern with control fell into stride.

"Big Iron," one of four Robbins originals on the album, is every Western you've ever seen fast-forwarded through the slow parts. An Arizona ranger and an outlaw named Texas Red meet in an unnamed town. Four minutes after the first charging guitar lick, a body lies dead in the street. It won't be the last one. Violence stalks the plains and lurks along the ridges. There are lynchings ("They're Hanging Me Tonight"), shootings ("Billy the Kid"), electrocutions ("The Master's Call"), buckings ("The Strawberry Roan"), more shootings ("Running Gun"), and a deadly cattle stampede ("Utah Carol"). A sense of resigned paranoia prevails.

The album, like many produced in Nashville in the late fifties and early sixties, shares a certain DNA with mid-nineties hip-hop, much of which channeled, sampled, and adapted personas from genre films—if not Westerns, then mafioso and Chinese wuxia classics, such as *Goodfellas* (1990) and *Master of the Flying Guillotine* (1976). Don Law, the Englishman who produced Robbins and like-styled artists, such as Bob Wills and Johnny Horton, was country music's RZA, its Dr. Dre. He not only crafted an indelible sound but also directed a kind of sonic cinema. *Gunfighter Ballads* was his *Deep Cover* (1992), his *Only Built 4 Cuban Linx . . .* (1995).

The deadly firefights on *Gunfighter Ballads* are interrupted by trail songs, oases in the action that also establish something of the stakes. In "A Hundred and Sixty Acres" and "The Little Green Valley," two cowboy standards, Robbins rhapsodizes about the comforts of home. His full-band take on Bob

Nolan's "Cool Water," led by a snake charm of a fiddle and with harmony provided by Tompall & the Glaser Brothers, foregrounds the song's thirst-driven delusions, making them all the more tantalizing. When Robbins croons the title phrase, drawing out the word "water" as if to wring it dry, you feel the disappointment. You taste it. It's the vocal equivalent of discovering that the Pepsi in your paper cup is tobacco spit.

The centerpiece of *Gunfighter Ballads* is "El Paso." Having put his deferential spin on the cowboy repertoire, Robbins tries to push the ball. If the other songs are black and white, "El Paso" arrives in Technicolor. The longest track on *Gunfighter Ballads*, it is also the most cinematic. To hear Robbins tell it, the song's narrative verve was characteristic of its composition. "I didn't know how it was going to end," he once told an interviewer. "It just kept on coming out, and coming out, and the tune was coming out at the same time. . . . I kept waiting for the end to come to see what was going to happen."

The setting is a place called Rose's Cantina. The narrator is a jealous, impulsive cowpoke. He's smitten with a dancer named Faleena, and he isn't alone. About a third of the way through "El Paso," a young cowboy comes into the bar and makes a move, and it's just too much for the narrator. Feeling threatened, he does the only thing he knows how to do: shoots the youngster dead in the street.

Most cowboy songs would end there, content to make a point about the hazards of unconsummated desire, but "El Paso" keeps going. The narrator steals a big horse and gallops to safety in New Mexico, and here again "El Paso" lets the tape run. The killer's rival might be dead, but Faleena is still living, and so, against his better instincts, he returns to El Paso, hoping that his heart might just win the day. Within eyeshot of the bar, five mounted cowboys open fire, yet still "El Paso" continues. Revived by the thought of Faleena twirling, the narrator, seriously wounded, manages to keep himself up in the saddle until he feels a "bullet go deep in my chest." This time he falls. As he takes his last breath, Faleena appears.

The last thing he feels before he passes away is the touch of her lips on his cheek.

"El Paso" features Grady Martin on guitar. Part of Nashville's A-team, a group of session musicians known for their versatility and technical precision, Martin played on Roy Orbison's "Oh, Pretty Woman," Loretta Lynn's "Coal Miner's Daughter," Lefty Frizzell's "Saginaw, Michigan," and Patsy Cline's "Walkin' after Midnight." He was part of Hank Williams's band, the Drifting Cowboys, but Hank never really let him cut loose. On "El Paso," which Martin would also record for his 1965 solo record, *Instrumentally Yours*, he picks a mean, meandering Spanish guitar. The nylon strings dance all around Robbins's vocals, as if taunting the narrator, spinning a web.

I suppose the song is about love and revenge and frustrated desire, but in truth, it's all in Robbins's performance, a marvel of overcommitment. "El Paso" is a cowboy ballad all right, but it's a mid-twentieth-century cowboy ballad, which is to say it's a tribute not to the West and not really even to Western movies but rather (not unlike Levinthal's photograph) to the imagination that lies under the Western's spell. There's a postwar disorientation to Robbins's surrender to his material. A sense of denial, personal as well as aesthetic, inflects his fervor. Fear of the future, after all, is the flip side of nostalgia. In light of V-E Day, in light of Elvis, Robbins seems to ask without asking: What does it mean to be a country singer? What does it mean to be an American man?

That there is something slightly juvenile about "El Paso"— and for that matter, the whole of *Gunfighter Ballads*—is a given. There are reasons why Rosie, aged five and in stubborn custody of a legit southern accent despite our Chicagoland digs, wants to listen to it on the regular—more so than, say, the Louvin Brothers' *My Baby's Gone* (1960) or Lucinda Williams's *Car Wheels on a Gravel Road* (1998), both of which keep Robbins company in the glove box. She is genuinely invested in the fates of Robbins's characters: Faleena, Texas

Red, Billy the Kid. Unlike so much of the kids' music and Disney soundtracks she requests but that I can't stomach, Robbins's polished collection of character-driven story songs is engaging enough on its face, even if the face also functions as a mask.

"El Paso" went to no. 1 on both the country and pop charts in January 1960. It won the Grammy for best country song the following year. Hippies, hillbillies, and even metalheads adopted the track. The Grateful Dead covered it in concert for three decades, and groups from Metallica to the Killers performed versions on the Texas leg of their tours. In 2014, *Rolling Stone* listed "El Paso" among the hundred greatest country songs of all time.

Even as the song found other suitors, "El Paso" kept working on Robbins, so much so that he recorded a sequel in 1966, and yet another installment a decade after that. Called "El Paso City," the third song in the trilogy is written from the perspective of a plane passenger who, while flying over the Texas border, is reminded of the first time he heard the original.

But Robbins isn't fooling anybody. He's singing about himself. History might be the great cure for nostalgia, but it's fun to imagine how life might have been better, more exciting, in another age. By being so out of step with the times, Robbins was actually perfectly in step with them. Unable to register the present, let alone predict the future, he looked back until the looking back became something worth singing about.

"Can it be," Robbins sings,

that man can disappear
From life and live another time
And does the mystery deepen 'cause you think
That you yourself lived in that other time?

The toy outfitted in cowboy clothes becomes the cowboy. From a certain distance, it's tough to tell the singer from the song.

HYMNS IN A WOMAN'S LIFE

Among the first songs I remember hearing are the hymns my great-grandmother sang: "I'll Fly Away," "Do Lord," "I Am Bound for the Promised Land." Doubtless I had heard other hymns before these, and still others with greater frequency, but to this day when I think of hymns, it is my great-grandmother who comes to mind.

Her name was Elmay (pronounced "Elmy"). I called her Mammaw Ray. She lived in a holler in West Virginia, on land owned by the company for which my great-grandfather dug coal. We would see them twice, maybe three times a year, once at their house on Thanksgiving, and at least once at my grandparents' place in Nashville, where they visited for a couple of weeks each summer.

I was the first of the fourth generation of the family and, being the oldest by several years, spent considerable time with my great-grandmother, much of it alone. I liked her. She was very short, and I suspect her height had much to do with my affection for her. Grownups were tall, which typically meant remote, but from an early age, she and I were within range.

Her blue eyes were big and blurry behind thick bifocals. Her hair, once blonde, had thinned and faded to a smoky white. She was the oldest woman I'd ever met, the oldest person alive for all I knew, but in retrospect, she wasn't so ancient. She'd had her children young, and they'd had their children young, and those kids, the first in the family to go to college (my mother among them), the first to never once set foot inside a coal mine, had had children too. As a result, she'd become a great-grandmother while still in her eighth decade.

Mostly, she sat in chairs, which is not to say she was idle. While the men hunted squirrels or stood around tailgates telling stories, she shucked corn, peeled potatoes, snapped beans, and stitched quilts. While she worked, between chatter about the weather and what I wanted to be when I grew up, she sang hymns.

In particular, she sang hymns about Heaven. "I'll fly away, Oh Glory." "There's a land that is fairer than day." "When we've been there ten thousand years, / Bright shining as the sun." Her voice was quiet. In a mountain accent, dulcet for all its strange diphthongs, she spoke more than sang the words. She had them from memory, which is to say by heart. At times they seemed almost as natural, as necessary, as breath.

Filled with glassy seas and golden shores and mansions outshining the sun, her hymns, it struck me even as a child, described places that were unfamiliar to her. She came from Appalachia, from hills and hollers, creeks and caves. The nearest sea was four hundred miles away. The sky was just a wedge between two mountains. Even in summer, sunshine was scarce.

Like the land, she was well-acquainted with shadows. I knew the stories. How every morning she'd send her husband into the mountain darkness. How every second of every day she tried not to listen for the bell, the ringing of which meant the worst had happened, a collapse in the tunnel, an explosion in a shaft. In the evening she filled a wooden tub with well water she'd heated over fire. From my great-grandfather's hair, face, neck, and arms, she washed and washed the rank coal dust that never fully washed away.

She kept bees, kept chickens, kept hillside gardens, kept a good heart. It was a matter of survival. My grandfather was the oldest of six: five sons and a daughter. When weather or economics shuttered the colliery and the miners traveled north to find work in factories, my grandmother's family (her future in-laws) dropped leftovers by the house anonymously, so worried were they that the children might starve.

What did hymns mean to my great-grandmother? How did they figure into her hard life? Was it nostalgia that endeared them to her memory? Was singing them just one of many mindless ways to while away the time?

In his essay "Hymns in a Man's Life," D. H. Lawrence confesses to an abiding love for church songs. "They mean to me almost more than the finest poetry," Lawrence writes, "and they have for me a more permanent value, somehow or other." For Lawrence, a coal miner's son who grew up attending a Congregationalist church but no longer counted himself among the believers, the power that hymns continued to exert over him was a source of amusement.

In the end, it isn't their faculty for inspiration, let alone their spiritual import, that make hymns indelible to Lawrence. It's their capacity to generate what he calls "wonder." The mere look and sound of certain words and phrases from the hymnbook—"sun of my soul," "lake of Galilee," "beauty of holiness"—fill Lawrence with a sense of absentminded awe. "I don't know what the 'beauty of holiness' is exactly," he writes. "But if you don't think about it—and why should you?—it has a magic."

I cannot say for sure, but for my great-grandmother, I think something like the opposite was true. It wasn't mainly aesthetics, sentimentality, or wonder for wonder's sake, that made hymns about Heaven so dear to her. It was the hope they articulated, the future they described. It was their promise of a better life than the one she deserved or had endured. It was their assurance of a final judgment and of an eternal rest, one that she believed awaited her, as one of her favorite hymns put it, on "the farther shore."

The summer I turned eight years old, my family took a trip to Florida. We rented a passenger van and drove down from Tennessee. It was a big deal because my great-grandparents came with us. It was their first time to see the sea. The morning after we arrived, my great-grandmother took me for a walk on the beach. I can still picture her now. She's barefoot in the sand. Her pants are rolled. Her heavy arms are hanging by her side. The breeze presses against her hair. Through her glasses, thick as ever, she is gazing out at the expanse, at the water, at the sky, at all that blue.

She didn't sing then; she was silent. It was as if, there at the edge of the land near the end of her life, she had stepped inside the hymns she'd carried with her, tuning her heart by them all the while and focusing her faith, which at that moment seemed very close to sight.

MR. BROOKS

I saw Garth—that's what we called him, Garth—when I was in the fourth grade, maybe fifth. He was touring in support of his 1993 *In Pieces* album. Although I had been listening to country for as long as I could listen, Garth was the artist that had turned me into an enthusiast. My grandfather had had Johnny Cash; my parents, Alabama. But Garth, Garth was mine.

As far as my folks were concerned, I could have him. When the guitar arpeggio at the start of "Friends in Low Places," his first hit, came over the radio, my father would switch the dial from 97.9, which played top 40 country, to talk radio or classic rock. "Blame it all on my roots / I showed up in boots," Garth sang, in a lyric that seemed to announce a changing of the guard, "And ruined your black-tie affair."

My father didn't own a black tie, but neither did he much wear boots. Something about Garth needled him. What I heard as brave and original, he heard as bigheaded, crude. Garth was one of those figures. A line in the sound. There was before and after: BG and AG.

His songs could be moving ("The Dance"), suspenseful ("The Thunder Rolls"), clever ("Full House"), scandalous ("That Summer"), even enlightened ("We Shall Be Free"), but for all their emotional and thematic range, they were bound by a fervor and intensity that was uniquely his own. Early reviews called his music "bawdy," "self-aggrandizing," "disturbing," and "hollow." You bought into it or you didn't.

I, for one, was invested. Garth's rise from "Friends in Low Places" (1990) had loosely coincided with my grandfather's willingness to let me cut his lawn unassisted, and so I saved the money I earned from mowing, as well as from painting the fences around his pasture, to buy *Ropin' the Wind* (1991) and then *The Chase* (1992) on cassette tape.

Both were sensations. In the spring of 1992, *The Chase* had debuted at no. 1, not only on the country charts, but on the pop charts as well, crowding out Madonna's *Erotica*, brushing shoulders with Whitney Houston's *Bodyguard* soundtrack. The album went nine times platinum. But I didn't know about that. I mounted the tractor, adjusted the headphones, and punched play on my portable tape player. By the time I last-lapped the backfield, having paused only long enough to refill the gas tank and flip the tape, I had listened to the album three or four times.

For all its flamboyance, I sensed in Garth's music a familiar intimacy. At heart, the man was a raconteur. The stories he spun in songs such as "The Thunder Rolls," "That Summer," and "Papa Loved Mama," which climaxes with a trucker crashing his big rig into his unfaithful wife's motel room, were every bit as detailed as they were overblown.

Garth might have been in the business of crashing black-tie affairs, but I thought he'd have been right at home sitting around the table on my grandfather's porch or in the passenger seat of my uncle's pickup on one of those drives when the road and the clock melted away in a space-time warp of narrative.

In theory at least, a close run-in with Garth wasn't out of the question. In early elementary school, a rumor circulated that he'd bought a farm on a hill over Old Dickerson Pike. We passed by the property every day going to and from school. You couldn't see much of the house, a two-story antebellum number, from the road, but there was a great big warehouse-looking structure off to the side, into which you could have easily fit a stage, a studio, a fleet of sports cars, or all of the above.

It wasn't possible, but if Garth really was up there, it meant that occasionally he had to come down, meant that to get to wherever he was going, the gate would have to open, and he'd turn onto the very road we were driving on. It wasn't possible, but then, one morning on our commute, we thought we might have passed him riding by us on a John Deere tractor, but it really wasn't possible, and then one night he and his family were walking out of Cracker Barrel as we were walking in, and it wasn't possible except that apparently it was. Suffice to say that by the time I came by a copy of *In Pieces*, this time on CD, Garth's music had gone from being a private excitement to a source of pride. He'd become Garth. Not Garth as in Prince or Pavarotti, not Garth as in a mononymous abstraction, but Garth as in I felt as if I knew him. To my mind, we were on a first-name basis.

A student in my mother's class had given her a "compact disc" player, and not knowing what to do with it, she'd lugged it home and left it sitting behind the chair in the den. I plugged it in and, over the course of a week, put to mind the entirety of *In Pieces*, from the first lines of the rousing "Standing Outside the Fire"—

We call them cool,
Those hearts who have no scars to show

—and the bridge of "Callin' Baton Rouge":

Hello, Samantha dear, I hope you're feeling fine
And it won't be long until I'm with you all the time

—to the final verse of the acoustic "Cowboy Song":

So when you see the cowboy, he's not ragged by his choice
He never meant to bow them legs
Or put that gravel in his voice

The sixth track, "Ain't Goin' Down ('Til the Sun Comes Up)," gave me fits. It was a barnburner, the fastest song I'd ever heard. It made "The Devil Went Down to Georgia" feel like a waltz. The song's laser-quick tempo took cues from the lyrics, which recounted the story of a redheaded girl's curfew-testing tear across a small southern town, and it was pure action, a lightning strike of verbs relayed lickety-split through a derecho of fiddles. In the CD booklet, the first verse looked like this:

> Six o'clock on Friday evenin'
> Momma doesn't know she's leavin'
> 'Til she hears the screen door slammin'
> Rubber squealin', gears ajammin'
>
> Local country station just ablarin' on the radio
> Pick him up at seven and they're headin' to the rodeo
> Momma's on the front porch screamin' out her warnin'
> Girl you better get your red head
>
> Back in bed before the mornin'

It sounded more like:

> Sixo'clockonFridayevenin'
> mommadoesn'tknowshe'sleavin'
> 'Tilshehearsthescreendoorslammin'
> rubbersquealin'gearsa-jammin'
> localcountrystationjustablarin'ontheradio
> pickhimupatsevenandthey'reheadin'totherodeo
> momma'sonthefrontporchscreamin'outherwarnin'
> girlyoubettergetyourredhead
> backinbedbeforethemornin'

And went on that way for three more verses. Garth was flouting rules even as he left few doubts that he could keep them. On an album whose title and cover art suggested quiet introspection, the song amounted to an exalting taunt. Go on, it said, see if you can.

I must have listened to "Ain't Goin' Down ('Til the Sun Comes Up)" fifty times, holding down the rewind button to revisit botched lines and then inevitably pressing too hard and having to scan forward from the start. Unlike the run-of-the-mill country songs on the radio, you couldn't passively absorb this one. You had to engage. Getting it down felt like an accomplishment. You carried it, flaunted it, like a favorite scar.

The skipping back and forth must have driven my parents up the wall, and yet, for all their disdain, I don't recall their ever asking me to stop. The concert, however, was a harder sell. The music wasn't at issue as much as the logistics. Did I have money to pay for the ticket? Thanks to the lawn mower, I did. Would there be adult supervision? Chad Cunningham's mom had volunteered to take us. And besides, why did I need to go *now*—wouldn't there be plenty of other chances to see Garth? Maybe so, I said, paraphrasing another Garth song, but what if tomorrow never comes?

It felt like a coup. Like Braves' baseball, *Mortal Kombat*, and our grandfather's stories, Garth was an enthusiasm I shared with my buddies. His music and proximity had given us a sense of privilege. We felt as if we'd found ourselves at the center of something special. The concert would serve as confirmation.

Or so we hoped. The truth was, I'd never been to a proper concert. The little live music I'd witnessed firsthand had come out of modest spaces: restaurants, churches, school gyms. On TV, I'd watched a music video in which Garth danced and sang in front of a rowdy crowd. I'd never seen anything like it. Unlike other country singers who stood flat-footed in front of microphones, Garth was a performance artist. He entered into his songs, acted them out. He was one of the first country singers to ditch a mic stand for a headset. It made the music video look more like Broadway, more like WWF, than the Grand Ole Opry. Even so, I didn't quite register as real what I witnessed on the screen. It might as well have been a Saturday morning cartoon.

As we parked and then hoofed it across the asphalt for what seemed like miles, any expectations I harbored deep down began to give way. The basketball arena soared up against the night sky. The ticket line spiraled around the building and spiraled some more. Once inside, we climbed and climbed flights of stairs and scooted across aisles before finally arriving at our seats. There were people everywhere. Above us, below us, pooled along the floor, crammed into the corners. "Garth!" they chanted, "Garth! Garth! Garth!"

Who were these people? Where had they come from? What did they think they knew about Garth? I stood there among them, hating them, feeling already as if a treasure had been pinched from me and distributed at random, one of thousands and thousands and yet wanting for some reason to be the only one. As it grew louder I grew quieter, stiller. By the time the lights dimmed and the music started, I stood encased in a thick cocoon of silence.

Garth shot from the stage. He really was electric. Part troubadour, part trapeze artist, he smashed guitars and slung cymbals, leapt over flames, climbed a rope ladder and swung out over the crowd. He did "I've Got Friends in Low Places," did "Papa Called Mama" and "Ain't Goin' Down ('Til the Sun Comes Up)," and I knew every word of every song but, swallowed by the crowd and struck dumb by the spectacle, could not bring myself to make a sound.

In one of his early songs, Garth had sung about burning bridges "one by one." Musically, though, he was in the business of building them, of connecting—or of at least fortifying the existing ties between—country and rock 'n' roll, country and pop, even country and rap.

I mean, sonically, how big a leap was "Ain't Goin' Down" to Alanis Morisette's "One Hand in My Pocket"? How much farther did you have to go to get to Outkast's "Player's Ball"? Already there, in seed form, was the country rap that the Luke Bryans and Florida Georgia Lines would steer into the mainstream a couple of decades later, just as Garth's admix of personality and spectacle portended the rise of a Carrie Underwood and a Taylor Swift.

Garth corralled exhilaration and derring-do into country music. He stampeded the genre out into the spotlight. It was thrilling, and it was exhausting. If there was something slightly comic about Garth, it was the comedy of misplacement, of those boots tracking the manure in among the black ties. And if there was something tragic about him, it came from a similar source. Why did he feel the need to show up there in the first place? What business does a country boy have in a ballroom? Who, in the end, were we trying to impress?

Whatever else it did, the concert forever altered my perception of Garth. He was, I realized, a very big deal. On those previous occasions when I'd seen him around, I hadn't thought about getting his autograph. I hadn't felt as if I needed it, not when I had the music, not when the man himself was right there. But the next time I saw him, a year or so later, out to eat with my family at a meat and three, I worked up the courage and walked over to the table where he was sitting with his wife and daughters.

"Mr. Brooks," I said, blushing, brandishing forth my father's pen, "would you do me the favor of signing my napkin?"

"You can call me Garth," he said.

"Thank you, Mr. Brooks," I repeated.

I never called him Garth again.

EVERYBODY'S BREAKING
SOMEBODY'S HEART

Several summers ago, I took my high school best friend, who was going through a divorce at the time, to see a concert at Nashville's Ryman Auditorium. I say "concert," but in reality, it was one of those Grand Ole Opry–style revues in which a few artists play two or three songs apiece and then call it a night. The bill was long, sundry, and strange. It included the songwriter Jimmy Webb ("Wichita Lineman," "MacArthur Park"), the Country Music Hall of Fame member Connie Smith, a three-year-old mandolin player, an indie rock band from New Zealand, Glen Campbell's kids, and Eric Church, who was joined on stage by Chris Stapleton and Little Big Town for a cover of the Band's "The Weight."

Church was the main draw. One of Nashville's leading men, he'd recently released an album that embraced hard rock riffs and spoken word poetry, in addition to nostalgic reminiscences of the Talladega Superspeedway. On one eight-minute track, he rails against the very Ryman stage on which he was set to perform. "No matter how satisfied her scream sounds," he says, "she always wants someone new." I wondered whether Church, in his sunglasses and leather jacket, would go there during his set, whether he'd make nice or cause a scene. I told my friend, who'd never been to the Ryman, about how Johnny Cash had smashed out the footlights with a microphone stand in 1965. I wondered whether we might be in for a repeat.

I was talking about music to keep from talking about things I didn't know how to talk about. My friend's wife had left him. There was another man involved. It had all come as a surprise. Despite growing up in Nashville, my friend had never been a country music fan. At the very least, I thought the show, for as long as it lasted, might take his mind off his troubles. I thought it might even give him a song or two to help him deal with his pain. What else is country music good for if not consoling the brokenhearted? What is it about if not the inevitability of ending up alone?

More than Church, the singer I was looking forward to seeing, the name that had made me want to buy tickets in the first place, was Charley Pride. I resorted to superlatives to try to pique my buddy's interest. Pride's voice, I told him, was one of the signature instruments in country music. Its sophisticated twang, equal parts brass and bass fiddle, was the fruit of a uniquely American climb. Pride's parents had been sharecroppers in Mississippi. He'd served in the army. In the Negro leagues, he'd pitched for the Memphis Red Sox and the Birmingham Black Barons, becoming a two-time all-star, before cutting a country demo that caught the ear of Chet Atkins, the guitar wonder turned RCA record executive.

In a genre that had deep roots in Black music but had never been particularly receptive to Black musicians, Pride went on to sell more records for RCA than any artist besides Elvis. He sent more than fifty singles into the *Billboard* country chart's top 10—thirty of them to no. 1. He was the second Black member of the Grand Ole Opry and in 2000 became the first Black artist inducted into the Country Music Hall of Fame.

"You ever hear 'Kiss an Angel Good Morning'?" I asked my friend. "How about 'Crystal Chandeliers'?" If any two songs could win a skeptic to country music, surely it was those two Pride standards, the first a spellbound ditty about the duties of romance, the second a cutting but good-hearted indictment of its shortfalls. Few singers could swing between warring sentiments with such aplomb. No other country artist after Patsy Cline had so elegantly surveyed the fraught landscape of love.

It was 10 p.m. The Ryman was just about full. A country-music award show had just ended at the hockey arena down the hill. Stragglers from there and the Broadway honky-tonks were drifting in drunk and tired but grateful, at that late hour, to have somewhere decent to go. We were seated on the main floor, in a pew to the left of the stage. Like a shaman, Marty Stuart, who had organized the concert and presided over it as emcee, began the show by summoning the spirits of country music's past. "This is the Mother Church," he said, "and if you feel something funny on your shoulders, it's just one of the ghosts of the greats."

Stuart and his band, the Fabulous Superlatives, did a Marty Robbins cover, and then a duo from Maryland called the Brothers Osborne did a Merle Haggard cover, and the mood was surreal, a touch spooky even, when Pride, who'd toured with Robbins and been inducted into the hall of fame by Haggard, made his entrance. It was as if all of Stuart's talk about ghosts and greats had worked a materializing magic that in turn exposed his shtick as hooey. The greats don't have ghosts, Pride's presence seemed to announce, because the greats never die.

Pride wore black pants and a black short-sleeved button-down with white tennis shoes. He looked like a retired general, in control even when at ease. He'd always set his own code. Somewhere I'd seen a photo of him standing in front of a picture of Hank Williams. Hank wore a cowboy hat. Pride donned a leisure suit and gold chains. I slapped my friend on the back. "This is going to be good," I said. I waited for the familiar guitar lick that tees up the first verse of "Kiss an Angel Good Morning."

> Whenever I chance to meet
> Some old friends on the street
> They wonder how does a man
> Get to be this way

Or for Pride to belt out the a cappella "Oh" at the maudlin start of "Crystal Chandeliers." But when the music started, I didn't recognize the song. Pride walked right up to the edge of the stage, which was crowded with musicians and instruments and wires. He lifted the microphone to his mouth with both hands. No sooner had he started singing than he seemed to lose the thread. He walked to the other end of the stage, the music still playing behind him, and when the chorus arrived, he lifted the mic to his mouth once more. But the words wouldn't come. The band made adjustments. Pride paced back and forth, less sure on his feet now, searching for the lyrics, occasionally letting out broken snatches of song under his breath.

A round of applause ensued. Several people on the main floor stood up and started cheering, thinking, perhaps, that what he needed was a little encouragement, that if he knew the crowd was on his side, he would be able to refocus or maybe feel appreciated enough to move on. But it was clear that he wasn't going to quit, not yet, clear that the song had become a challenge from which he refused to back down. He tried the chorus again, but when it came time to move into the next verse, he just shook his head and let out something like a sigh. The band kept playing, a little quieter now, their poses more wooden, trying and failing to hide their concern.

Questions crowded my mind. It dawned on me that the intense feeling and emotional vulnerability that characterized Pride's music emanated from its opposite. His vocal performances were commanding, nearly perfect, and this allowed the cracks in the relationships he sang about to cut through. It took a lot of sense to sing about senseless romance. It took a lot of confidence to sell weakness the way he did.

This time, though, Pride the performer was superseding Pride's songbook. It was as if, in the course of a few minutes, he had exposed country music, with its allegiance to down-and-outers and loss and shame, for a ruse. Finally, after what felt like an hour crushed into five minutes, Pride gave up on the song. The drums pattered out; the guitars faded. While the music had been going, there had been the possibility of a rally. Now that the stage was quiet, there was no place for him to hide.

Suddenly, I felt terrible for subjecting my friend to what, I assumed, must have seemed like a sad display of incompetence by a washed-up has-been. So I stood up and made to leave. When my friend didn't follow, I motioned in his direction, only to be met by the most unexpected sight. There he sat, staring up at Charley Pride in a kind of rapture. He was neither horrified nor annoyed. Unlike me, he wasn't ready to make an escape. He looked worried, moved, and utterly consumed. There was nothing that could have broken his concentration. I wondered what Pride looked like from his vantage. We had been sitting on the same pew, but he was watching, I realized, a different performance. It was as if his hurt and confusion and whatever else he'd experienced and survived had given him, for all that it had taken, a fresh access of empathy, as if in Pride's onstage struggles, he'd glimpsed traces of his own.

There was a song being sung between them that I couldn't quite trace. "A spirit ditty," as Keats wrote, "of no tone." It was something about what happens when the sure things fly out from under us, about where we land after what we've taken for granted takes us for a ride. "Everybody's breaking somebody's heart," it might have gone, "but I never thought you'd be the one to break mine."

Pride was stubborn. You had to be to do what he'd done in his life and music. He wasn't going to exit the stage without putting up a fight. I settled back into the pew just as the band started playing again. The people around us clapped. "We love you, Charley," someone shouted from the balcony. My buddy looked over at me and smiled. He nodded toward the stage. Together we waited for what would come, for the singing, for the silence, for the stammer in between, for whatever pride sounds like on the other side of shame.

LONESOME TOGETHER

On YouTube there's a rare video of Johnny Cash and Kris Kristofferson performing the song "Sunday Mornin' Comin' Down." The segment, which was taped in Los Angeles as part of a 1978 prime-time special, made for a very public reunion—it had been nine years since Cash first performed Kristofferson's song on *The Johnny Cash Show*, his short-lived TV variety program featuring rock, blues, and folk singers alongside the Grand Ole Opry crowd.

The original performance had been controversial. Cash's producers, anticipating blowback from the song's references to drug use, had asked him to switch the chorus from "On a Sunday mornin' sidewalk / I'm wishing, Lord, that I was stoned" to "On a Sunday mornin' sidewalk / I'm wishing, Lord, that I was home." Cash said he'd give it some thought, but when the time came, he delivered the lines as is, putting the weight of his quavering bass-baritone behind a lyric that was at once a provocation (drugs were a Nashville taboo) and a personal confession (Cash really was hooked on pills). A live recording of the performance was released to country radio and quickly ran up the charts, eventually winning Kristofferson the 1970 CMA award for Song of the Year.

The success of "Sunday Mornin'" was a windfall for Kristofferson. An army helicopter pilot with a degree from Oxford, he had recently resigned from a teaching gig at West Point to hawk country songs in Nashville. To make rent, he took a job as a janitor at Columbia Studios, where Cash had recorded hit after hit: "Ring of Fire," "Understand Your Man," "The Ballad of Ira Hayes." Cash was only four years older than Kristofferson, only a couple inches taller, yet his fame and panache, paired with the guttural elegance of his pipes, gave him a magnetic otherworldliness. Dressed in black, cocking his six-string like a shotgun, he was part prophet, part phantom, part live wire.

At Cash's memorial concert in 2003, Kristofferson likened him to a panther. "He was dark, dangerous," Kristofferson said, "a force of nature, absolutely electric and absolutely unpredictable." What Kristofferson admired in Cash was a certain strength of character that masqueraded as unconcern. "He's a walkin' contradiction, partly truth and partly fiction," Kristofferson writes in "The Pilgrim, Chapter 33," "Takin' ev'ry wrong direction on his lonely way back home."

As he swept the floors, Kristofferson studied his hero. He slipped demos to Cash's wife, June Carter, and when that failed, he procured an army national guard helicopter and landed it on Cash's waterfront lawn. Such antics might very well have earned him a restraining order were it not that "Sunday Mornin'," included on the demo, was tailor-made for Cash. The song tapped into his outlaw persona while also spotlighting the growing hitch in his strut. It was one of those recordings that felt both gutsy and auspicious, as if the last country song you'd expect Johnny Cash to sing was the one country song Cash alone could sell. The conceit is simple enough. A man wakes up late and goes for a trot, not unlike the situation described in the Beatles' "A Day in the Life," released two years earlier, in 1967: "Woke up, fell out of bed / Dragged the comb across my head."

But if the Beatles' psychedelic classic satirizes the banality of modern ritual, "Sunday Mornin'" sets out to revivify the mundane. The movements of the Beatles' character are automatic, the mindless routines of a middling banker or bureaucrat. But there is nothing pat about the actions of Kristofferson's subject. His alarm clock is a hangover headache. He doesn't drink coffee; he sips the hair of the dog. He forgoes a suit and tie for his "cleanest dirty shirt." His morning walk is like a cold shower. His senses sharpen and coruscate. He hears songs issuing from a nearby church, smells fried chicken, sees kids swinging in the park, and finds himself transported to "something that he lost somehow, somewhere along the way." The bells ringing in the distance echo like "disappearing dreams." Above all, his jaunt underscores his isolation. "There's something about a Sunday," Kristofferson writes, "That makes a body feel alone."

Like all great writers, Kristofferson quarried his own experience for materials. Ostensibly, "Sunday Mornin'" was about Kristofferson, a struggling upstart who, as the opening verse describes, had "smoked his brain the night before / With cigarettes and songs that I'd been pickin'." But the scenario he sketches, for all its idiosyncrasy, was pliable enough for Cash, whose struggles had to do with fame instead of obscurity, to fashion into his own image.

Although Cash was a formidable songwriter himself—he penned "Folsom Prison Blues," "I Walk the Line," "Big River," and "Tennessee Flat-Top Box," to name a few—his greatest talent was interpretation. Kristofferson's spare, bluesy version of "Sunday Mornin'," recorded for his 1970 solo debut, is the dawn-crack moan of a cocksure talent who has failed to catch his big break. Cash speeds up the tempo, adds horns and strings, and in so doing morphs "Sunday Mornin'" from a song about the loneliness of being on the bottom into a song about the loneliness of being at the top. In the sixties, Cash had stomped out the lights at the Grand Ole Opry, set fire to a swath of national forest, and been arrested for smuggling painkillers across the Mexican border. His "Sunday Mornin'" was like the hangover Sabbath it described: visceral, rueful, not quite repentant.

The success of "Sunday Mornin'" allowed Kristofferson to hang up the broom. In the months and years that followed, Waylon Jennings, Bobby Bare, Faron Young, Roger Miller, and Janis Joplin cut songs by Kristofferson, who in turn found a larger audience for his own records. Buoyed by the single "Why Me?"—a pseudospiritual that found Kristofferson reflecting on the unlikeliness of his good fortune—his 1972 album, *Jesus Was a Capricorn*, went to no. 1.

Next came Hollywood. Kristofferson, who paired flinty good looks with a drifter's devil-may-care, starred with James Coburn and Bob Dylan in Sam Peckinpah's brilliant *Pat Garrett and Billy the Kid* and won a Best Actor Golden Globe for his 1976 role alongside Barbra Streisand in *A Star Is Born*. At the taping of Cash's special, he was in the middle of filming a TV special in Natchez, Mississippi, with Muhammad Ali.

For Cash, however, the seventies became something of a wilderness. The inner conflict teased in "Sunday Mornin'" intensified. There were rehab stints and relapses. There was an earnest return to Christian faith. His musical output was frequent, if often forgettable. In addition to run-of-the-mill collections of original material, he cut patriotic concept albums, covers of country standards, and regurgitations of old hits. The landmark early albums were decades behind him, and the miraculous final recordings were still decades away. At the airing of the 1978 performance of "Sunday Mornin'," Kristofferson was forty-two, a still rising star. Cash, forty-six, was a portrait of the country artist as an aging man.

Even so, there is little in the YouTube video to suggest that Kristofferson has outgrown his awe, and even less to suggest that Cash harbors feelings of resentment. He introduces Kristofferson as "one of the biggest stars in the world." Kristofferson's halting entry onstage, however, shows that he is under no delusions about who is standing in whose shadow. Just how indebted he feels to Cash becomes clear in the banter that follows. "I loved it, and I sang it, and I've been singing it ever since," Cash says of "Sunday Mornin'." "Well, up till now," Kristofferson replies, "that was the proudest moment of my life, so this might just be the proudest."

The whole thing, repartee and all, is over in less than four minutes, and yet the song they sing is really the song of their lives, the song of a friendship as far-fetched as it seemed fated.

In the following years, that connection only deepened: they toured the world together as part of the supergroup the Highwaymen and grew closer still in the final months of Cash's life, when Kristofferson called to check on him nearly every day.

In the video, Cash takes the first verse with characteristic authority. Kristofferson takes the second with characteristic insouciance, coming in just late enough to make you wonder if, in his momentary amazement, he has forgotten the words, but not late enough to convince you that he's doing anything other than wheeling free. Their voices alternate, each moving at its own pace, each making its individual stride before falling into loose step at the chorus:

And there's nothing short of dyin'
That's half as lonesome as the sound
Of a sleepin' city sidewalk
And Sunday mornin' coming down

The wages of freedom are lonesomeness, but being lonesome together is not the same as being alone.

THE BALLAD OF TAYLOR
AND DREW

I knew the song wasn't about me. But when the singer said my name, I couldn't help it—against my better judgment, I felt called out, confronted. It's not every day you hear your name in a country song—in any song, country or otherwise—not when your name is Drew. Bobby, Billy, Sarah, sure. But not Drew. Drew, as a poet told me once when I handed him a book to sign after a reading, was a name best suited for mailmen, milkmen, and detectives.

I was none of the above. I was newly arrived in DC from Nashville. I was about to start a job at a magazine. Homesickness, big snake, had hung a fang on my heart. Listless on a lunch break one of my first days in the city, I had wandered into an art museum and found myself surrounded by Kodak Brownie photographs of barns, country stores, Baptist churches, family graveyards.

Year after year, starting in the mid-1970s, the artist, William Christenberry, had taken pictures of the same places, all of them in rural Alabama. A shack commanded the landscape in one picture. Two decades later, kudzu had swallowed it whole. The continuity of subject matter gave the images a highly neurotic yet documentary quality. There was loss in it. There was love. The photographs, some wall-sized, some more like windows, were accompanied by sculptures of the same structures, withdrawn from nature now, miniaturized, and presented on pedestals in haunting, idealized form. Christenberry called the models "Dream Buildings," "Southern Sculptures," "Memory Forms."

I was hooked. I returned to the show every damn day until it shuttered, dubious as to whether I had hit on a homecoming or a home burial or something else entirely but homing to the work all the same. What the pictures said was that the American South was changing. Yes, yes, but on the imagination of its exiles, the sculptures countered, the place retained an irrevocable hold.

To be sure, the South, or at least my Middle Tennessee sliver of it, had never had more of a hold on me. On the Metro train, between white spells of motion sickness, I was reading Randall Jarrell, poet, essayist, famous melancholic, a writer who, like me, hailed from Nashville, and who, for one reason or another, had hit the northern road. "Turn as I please, my step is to the south," Jarrell wrote in a poem called "90 North." Before, I had taken the line as a metaphor for the inevitable letdown that attends great accomplishment—in Jarrell's poem reaching the North Pole—but now I wondered whether, beneath the surface, Jarrell wasn't making a more fundamental statement about leaving home. It hounded you. It crawled up in your hair. In a sense, you weren't really from any place until you left.

As I blew around DC, not yet knowing whether I wanted to settle in, I found myself reaching for country music as if it were an aide memoire. It was no longer a diversion, no longer background noise. It had become a palliative to out-of-placeness and anonymity. Hearing the stuff carried me straight back, made me feel known again and safe enough.

To say that I had grown up listening to country music was an understatement. I had grown up in it, a tadpole in pond water. The music played more or less everywhere all the time, one song fading into another and then another, such that it became a kind of din, a lesser degree of silence, and at some point you quit paying attention to it until you got your head above water and started hearing it again.

My hearing, best as I could tell, had returned the morning I left for DC. It was late August. We were standing in the driveway at my grandparents' house. Everybody in the family had said their goodbyes except for my uncle, Steve, who stayed sitting in his idling truck under a magnolia tree, his arm hanging out the window, his black sunglasses making his disposition impossible to read.

Only when I started to get into my car did he tap on the horn and motion me over. I climbed into his truck and closed the door. "There's a track I want you to hear," he said and preceded to play a song by Kenny Chesney called "Back Where I Come From." After the last chorus, in which Chesney switches the lyrics from "Back where I come from, / Where I'll be when it's said and done" to "Back where I come from, / I'm an old Tennessean," Steve had lowered the volume, turned to me, his blue eyes spilling over the rim of his glasses, and issued a charge that was also a caution: "Don't you never forget where you come from, you hear?"

I had heard "Back Where I Come From" many times before, but I had never paid much attention to the words. Now I was all ears. I listened to the CD, which my uncle ejected and handed to me as a parting gift, over and over on my drive. In the song, Chesney sketches a pretty and utopian vision of his hometown. It's a place where "the clock ticks and the cattle graze," a place where kids erect beer can pyramids on riverbanks on Saturday nights and climb up the water tower to scrawl their name.

That I had never done these things—that Chesney, who, judging by his music, seemed to spend more time in the tropics than the sticks, might not have done them either—was beside the point. We had done them in theory. We certainly could have. Someday, we'd do them again. The song was like a fantasy about the future projected onto an intimation of the past. Country was wistful music for wistful people. I was arrested by the reverie, comforted by—which is to say distracted from—all that was about to change.

But there was something unnerving about that song with my name in it. It was called "Teardrops on My Guitar." The artist was a young shake-scene called Taylor Swift. The two-syllable, one-syllable rhythm of her name brought to mind the female ghosts of country music's past: Kitty Wells, Dottie West, Brenda Lee, Patsy Cline. But her take on the music was something else altogether.

Swift's first single, released a few months earlier, had been a coy ballad called "Tim McGraw." In that song, Swift confessed that her own favorite song was by the country singer Tim McGraw, and yet didn't once reveal what Tim McGraw song she had in mind. Was it "Indian Outlaw"? Or was it "Everywhere"? Was it "Getting Down on the Farm" or "Don't Take the Girl"? Tim McGraw could be charming. Tim McGraw could be cornball. You could probably tell a lot about a person by which Tim McGraw they preferred.

Without a doubt my favorite Tim McGraw song was "Just to See You Smile," a deceptively slight number about forcing happiness and contentment in front of an ex-lover. "And yesterday I knew just what you wanted," McGraw sings in the final verse,

When you came walkin' up to me with him
So I told you that I was happy for you
And given the chance I'd lie again

The song was a white lie, insisted on through an aching fake smile. It was McGraw at his archest and most self-aware, one of the few places where his congenital earnestness made room for earnest equivocation. I doubted Swift had "Just to See You Smile" in mind in "Tim McGraw," but if not "Just to See You Smile," then which one? Maybe "A Heart Don't Forget'? Maybe "Not a Moment Too Soon"?

Simpering aside, there was a confident assurance to Swift's evasion. "Tim McGraw," after all, was addressed to a "boy in a Chevy truck / That had a tendency of getting' stuck." The song wasn't for you. It was for him. This was country music as wink and nod. The point was that the boy in the truck knew the Tim McGraw song. He and Swift had apparently danced to it "all night long."

Then again, Swift's affinity for Tim McGraw made for its

own kind of reveal. It wasn't as if McGraw, always more competent heartthrob than singular talent, was in the canon. He was popular, sure. Diligent, if not ambitious, he flexed and finessed his modest strengths without ever breaking much of a sweat. Nearly fifteen years since he had first entered the Nashville scene, McGraw was still very much a presence on the radio and the stage, but he hadn't been anybody's hero, not until now. The fact of the matter was that Swift, sixteen when "Tim McGraw" hit the radio, hadn't grown up under the influence of Nashville's honky-tonk heroes. She'd grown up listening to Tim McGraw, who, along with his wife, Faith Hill, had commanded the charts in the late 1990s and early aughts. Paying tribute to him, Swift had also turned him into prologue.

If anything "Teardrops on My Guitar" was even savvier. As if anticipating flak for cutting in line, the song seemed intent on broadcasting Swift's country bona fides. The title alone fashioned a concise history of the genre. Had any title ever got to the crux of the art form more succinctly? I mean, what was country music if not just that: heartache banged out against a fret board?

The song had a sense of inevitability about it. You just knew that sooner or later someone would have written the lyric. But it was also clear that they wouldn't have written it quite like this. What Swift and cowriter Liz Rose did with the fated, flagrantly obvious sentiment was surprising. This wasn't cut-and-paste song crafting. For all its surface homage to classic country tropes, "Teardrops on My Guitar" bore the imprint of a clever wordsmith who wasn't about to shy from applying a timeless idea in a contemporary context, no matter how unconventional. The chorus seemed to channel Hank Williams's "There's a Tear in My Beer." Both songs took heartache as a cue. Both traced falling tears back to their sad source. But the similarities mostly served to spotlight the differences. Williams's sob fest was set in a smoky barroom. His narrator seemed to be shouldering a world of trouble. The song could very well have served as his last will and testament. Swift, alas, was singing about a teenage crush.

The music video for "Teardrops on My Guitar" was filmed at Hume Fogg High School, Randall Jarrell's alma mater. Perched on the hill between Seventh and Eighth Avenues, Hume Fogg was a stone's skip from Tootsie's, Robert's Western World, and the rest of the Lower Broadway honky-tonks where Willie Nelson and Lucinda Williams had once cut their chops. The Ryman Auditorium, Hank Williams's home away from home, was just around the corner. But Swift chose Hume Fogg. In her music, the bar stools and neon signs were ceding pride of place to the locker, the bleacher, the dining hall.

"Country music," V. S. Naipaul wrote in his essay about Nashville, "created a community and was the expression of a community." In other words, what you harkened to in Hank Williams's "There's a Tear in My Beer," at least in part, was the recognition of yourself and your own experience. It was a pervious border, the one between music and life. Hank was you and you were Hank. The music offered, among other things, a kind of validation. You weren't alone in your pain or your poverty. Things in your life, Hank swore and was beloved for swearing, could be a hell of a lot worse. But were you Taylor Swift? Could Taylor Swift ever be you?

You could dismiss "Teardrops on My Guitar" as mushy and melodramatic, but at some level you had to admire Swift's pluck. That she didn't have the harrowing backstory or world-weariness of a Loretta Lynn, that she didn't have the pure voice of, say, a Pam Tillis or a LeAnn Rimes, she compensated for with ardent circumspection about adolescence, which, in her conception of it, was as charged with emotional resonance as any of the divorces, depressions, infidelities, religious awakenings, and midlife crises that had given rise to the country music of old. Which is not to say that the travails of teenagers had been anathema to country before Swift came along. In "The Ballad of the Teenage Queen," Johnny Cash had narrated the story of a blue-eyed, Hollywood-bound young starlet's stubborn devotion to her small-town beau. Katie and Tommy, the pair of ill-starred high school lovers in Trisha Yearwood's "She's in Love with the Boy," make plans to get married against the wishes of Katie's father, who doesn't think Tommy—"When it comes to brains," the man says, "he got the short end of the stick"—is good enough for his daughter. In Tim McGraw's 2002 hit "Red Ragtop" (could that have been Swift's favorite?), the back seat of the titular cabriolet becomes the scene of a high school fling. In each of these songs juvenile romance is descried from a distance. Cash and Yearwood play the role of omniscient narrators. Even "Red Ragtop," though more of a personal reminiscence, is rendered as a hazy memory conjured by the sight of a similar car at a stoplight years and years after the fact.

In "Teardrops on My Guitar," it was as if Yearwood's Katie or Cash's nameless queen had stepped out of the song to speak for herself. At once more banal and more affecting than those picaresque visions of teenage romance, the song amounted to a refutation. For one, Swift's number was set in the present tense. For two, nothing really happened, which is what typically happens. The plot was as thin as the feelings were inflated. Nobody got engaged. Nobody got pregnant. Nobody ran off in the middle of the night to a drive-in movie let alone to Tinsel Town. It was, put simply, a song about being overlooked and little regarded. A song about awkward glances, fake smiles, silent longing, and being jealous and not knowing why. It just so happened that at the center of all this swooning and second-guessing was a boy named Drew.

When it came to names, country singers tended to reach for the old-fashioned (Vince Gill's "Liza Jane"), the hideous (the Oak Ridge Boys' "Elvira"), the striking (Dolly Parton's "Jolene"), and the clever (Johnny Cash's "A Boy Named Sue"). The idiosyncrasy of "Drew," a name that wasn't rare but wasn't exactly native to country music, gave texture to the song's broader, breezier strokes. Swift wasn't talking about boys in general. She had one boy in mind.

"Drew looks at me," she sings in the first verse. "Drew talks to me" in the second. "Drew walks by me" in the third. Drew was a heartbreaker. Drew was also oblivious. But Swift was cognizant of Drew's every word, especially the ones he confided to her about his girlfriend, a nameless character that she doesn't present as competition so much as a cipher for her own fantasies. "She better hold him tight," she sings in the final verse, "give him all her love, / Look in those beautiful eyes and know she's lucky."

Yes, the whole thing had the feel of a CW drama. In the video, Drew was played by an actor from *One Tree Hill*. Why, in other words, did I care? If Drew had been named John or Bill, would the song have made an impression? What if I was still living in Nashville instead of five hundred miles up the road?

I was hardly the only one to take notice. "Teardrops on My Guitar" spent more than six months on the country charts, rising all the way to number two and in the process tilling the soil for Swift's next single, an upbeat, eminently catchy tune called "Our Song" that would become her first of many no. 1 hits. Critics swooned. Stages opened. Kris Kristofferson would say of Swift, "She blows me away."

For me, though, a country boy mislaid in the big city and doomed as ever to try to read the world through songs, the blow was less a mighty wind than a fist in the gut. Name notwithstanding, I didn't think for a minute that Swift had written "Teardrops on My Guitar" about me. And yet, in a sense, I suspected she had indeed written the song about me, about saps like me who were prone to lean on country music for catharsis, when it was also, like some wrecked truck behind the house of a customer way overdue, just there for the taking, ready and waiting to be repossessed.

In the video, as in the lyrics, Swift clutched at a guitar. In so doing, she was assuming the posture of countless country singers who had come before her, from Hank Williams on down. She was one of them all right. And she wouldn't be beholden to them anymore than they had been beholden to their forebears. "Teardrops on My Guitar" was pop country and alt-country and confessional country and a hundred other qualifying adjectives that potentially disqualified it from being country all together. It was also the future of country, that much was clear.

Even so, I was iffy. Removed from Nashville, I wanted Nashville to look and sound like Nashville. I wanted the music to move south instead of north or west or in whatever direction Swift was pushing it. I wanted "Back Where I Come From," wanted my Dream Buildings, my Memory Forms. What I heard Swift saying was that the Nashville I left wouldn't be the Nashville I returned to, and that nostalgia was only a pretty word for denial.

Still, I couldn't shake "Teardrops on My Guitar." That was the catch, the way a song about being ignored could make you pay attention, the way a lyric about not being able to stop thinking about someone who didn't think much about you could insinuate itself into your thoughts until it became, as Drew had to Swift, "the song in the car you kept singing, don't know why you do."

I felt sorry for Drew. The joke was on him. He might have been the reason for the teardrops on Swift's guitar but was there any question about who, in the end, would have the bigger broken heart?

THE STUMP

In the song "This Is Country Music" from the album *This Is Country Music*, the country singer Brad Paisley characterizes country music as stubbornly countercultural. In music, in the free world, in the twenty-first century, you're not supposed to do and say this or that, Paisley sings, "But this is country music, and we do." The song is an apology and a plea, defensive and offensive in equal measure. "Do you like to drink a cold one on the weekend and get a little loud?" Paisley asks in the second verse, as if making a pitch to an iffy outsider:

Do you wish somebody had the nerve to tell that
    stupid boss of yours
To shove it next time he yells at you?

The idea is that country is music for real people with real problems. It may not be hip or sophisticated to make art to such practical ends, but country artists, Paisley insists, have never traded candor for cool. Are you sick and tired of your boss? Well, Johnny Paycheck, whose 1977 hit "Take This Job and Shove It" Paisley references, wrote the book on that. Country music understands.

Country, in the Paisley sense, doesn't denote a geographical region or even a particular sound so much as it represents a way of being in the world. Leave angst to indie rock, ambiance to EDM. Country is the province of the practicable. It doesn't meditate on existential despair; it narrates the bad fight and the bum job. It doesn't extract sacrifice from experience; it salutes, in Paisley's words, "the memory of those that died defending the old red, white, and blue." Country is down-to-earth music, of-the-earth music. If it mines the unsaid, it mines it in the palpable. "This is real," Paisley sings in the chorus. "This is your life in a song."

Or is it? The workaday definition insisted on in "This Is Country Music" chafes against the rather expansive notion put forward in the title song from Paisley's previous album, *American Saturday Night*. "She's got Brazilian leather boots on the pedal of her German car," that song begins:

> Listens to the Beatles singing back in the USSR
> Yeah she's goin' around the world tonight
> But she ain't leavin' here

"American Saturday Night" is an ode to ethnic multiplicity. It plays like the fulfillment of the dream laid out by Garth Brooks in "We Shall Be Free." Like that morale booster, "American Saturday Night" suggests, however covertly, that country music can transcend the mundane. It does more than reinforce stereotypes. No idea is off-limits. Country can be as large-minded and diffuse as the country, which in its heterogeneity can be, and often is, as big and diffuse as the world.

So which is it, the narrow road or the open gate? Is it parochial and proud of it, as in "This Is Country Music," or progressive, even visionary, as in "American Saturday Night"? Paisley, for his part, refuses to commit. His music airs and exploits both impulses with equanimity. In "Welcome to the Future," he summons memories of old friends and the ghosts of civil rights pioneers to marvel at the election of Barack Obama:

> I had a friend in school
> Running back on a football team
> They burned a cross in his front yard
> For asking out the homecoming queen

Then, in "Accidental Racist," he whines about the burden of white guilt via a conversation about the Confederate flag with a Black Starbucks barista.

In his attempt to both expand country music's horizons and fortify its borders, in his appeal to its better angels and its bitter demons, Paisley might just be the quintessential country artist. His great subject, insofar as a country star can be said to have one, is contradiction. Although he is one of the two or three best guitar players in Nashville, Paisley seldom strays too far from tried-and-true country melodies and arrangements. He's far too steeped in the genre to ever supersede it. Instead, his preferred mode of invention has been to bend country music back in on itself.

Paisley is a pro at revivifying old clichés. In "River Bank," from the album *Moonshine in the Trunk*, he twists bromides about summer R&R into clever commentary about social class. The phrase "laughing all the way to the bank" becomes, under Paisley's pen, "laughing all the way to the river bank." Who needs the lottery, the song contends, when the river is there for the taking?

The outdoors is one of Paisley's favorite subjects. "River Bank," for instance, eddies against "Water," a Paisley hit from a few years earlier, which, in situating water at the very center of southern life, from a child's "inflatable pool full of dad's hot air" to a wet T-shirt contest at Daytona Beach, seems almost to channel Philip Larkin's short poem of the same title. "If I were called in / to construct a religion," Larkin wrote,

> My liturgy would employ
> Images of sousing,
> A furious devout drench

The secularly spiritual, Larkin-like ecstasy of Paisley's "Water" says much about the preoccupations of contemporary country relative to the southern music of the past. In the hymns and gospel music from which the genre evolved, and which themselves did not evolve so much as spring wholesale from passages of the King James Bible, water, more often than not, was a place to commune with the divine.

"As I went down in the river to pray" begins a nineteenth-century spiritual, or sorrow song, that was repopularized by

Allison Krauss on the T Bone Burnett–produced *O Brother, Where Art Thou?* soundtrack:

Studyin' about that good ol' way
And who shall wear the starry crown?
Good Lord show me the way!

Water here symbolizes the washing away of sin and guilt. In storms and tribulations—"when," as another hymn puts it, "sorrows like sea billows roll"—water is what God parts and stills and comes walking across, or else what he stirs up and goes thundering through.

Indeed, the water that courses through so much of the country music of old is turbulent, rising. It conjures confusion instead of clairvoyance, torment instead of tranquility. The titles alone are telling: "Whispering Sea," "Five Feet High and Rising," "Lost on the River." "Come to my rescue," Don Gibson pleads in "Sea of Heartbreak," "Take me and keep me / Away from the sea." "Driftin' out across the blue ocean," counters Patsy Cline in "I'll Sail My Ship Alone," "Tho' all the sails you've torn, / And when it starts to sinkin', / I'll blame you." In these songs water is something to be rescued from or else buried under. The flood is the prevailing image. Collective consciousness is ribboned in a watermark.

In Paisley's "Water," however, beach and riverbank steadily beckon, and not as places of quiet contemplation, as in the case of a classic such as "Whispering Sea," which finds Loretta Lynn divulging a secret love to the waves she hopes will sweep her desire away. Water, in Paisley, is no longer a metaphor for revelation or upheaval. It's no longer the stage for tragedy. It's a vacation spot, plain and simple. "All you really need this time of year," Paisley sings,

Is a pair of shades
And ice cold beer
And a place to sit somewhere near
Water

Water is where you fish and flirt. It's where you find pure escape. It's not a mirror, not a marvel for that matter. It doesn't presage heaven any more than it foreshadows destruction. In the end, what Paisley's "Water" celebrates is leisure. Not the hard-earned kind, but the kind to which loafers tend to feel entitled. Country music, Paisley would have us believe, isn't concerned with struggle so much as relief. Ultimately, it's about where and how to spend capacious loads of free time.

But it's not entirely clear whether Paisley believes what he's preaching, whether he approves, objects, or is only making an observation, and if he is making an observation, whether it's an observation about country music or contemporary life in the South. In even his most ostensibly shallow songs, there is, to my ear, an undercurrent of cultural satire. Paisley's genius, from one song to the next, has been to fuse earnestness and irony into an ambivalence that is difficult to parse. Ever since a trio of songs from the early aughts found him satirizing reality TV stars ("Celebrity"), binge drinking ("Alcohol"), and internet chat rooms ("Online"), I don't quite know when to take Paisley at his word. Sincerity has a way of eluding even his most ardent love songs.

Are we, for instance, to believe the sentiment he expresses in a song such as "She's Everything," when, given the choice between his girl and going fishing, he chooses a rod and reel in "I'm Gonna Miss Her"? It raises the question: Could "Water," for all its apparent frankness, be a riff on the rash of contemporary country songs about vacation? That the song very well could be, but might not be at all, is a testament to Paisley's slipperiness. Either the joke is on listeners who have a tendency to read too deeply into lyrics, or the joke is on the casual hearer who thinks he's getting yet another straight-ahead summer beach song. Either way, someone, perhaps everyone, is getting nudged.

The contradictions that characterize Paisley's music spill into his off-stage persona. He toggles between teetotaling and casual drinking yet *Moonshine in the Trunk* is essentially a collection of carousing songs. Some of these numbers are evidently tongue-in-cheek. It's clear that Paisley the man isn't Paisley the narrator of "Crushin' It," a frat guy who is preternaturally gifted at smashing beer cans against his head. But is Paisley praising the antihero for his antic hedonism, or is he disparaging him?

Nowhere, to my ear, is Paisley's concern with hypocrisy and contradiction more furtive than in "This Is Country Music." The song could be alternatively titled, "Is This Country Music?" Every line feels like a provocation. "You're not supposed to use the word 'cancer' in a song," Paisley sings in the first line, "And tellin' folks that Jesus is the answer might rub 'em wrong." But does country music really do that? we wonder. Is it, as Paisley claims, evangelistic? And if the fuss it raises about Jesus does indeed offend, well then who's to blame, something in the culture or something in the sound? The songs that Paisley name drops just a few lines later only complicate things.

Chief among them is "Mama Tried," the Merle Haggard classic from 1968, the narrative of which is anchored not by an acceptance but rather a rejection of Christian faith:

Despite all my Sunday learnin'
Towards the bad I kept on turnin'
'Til Mama couldn't hold me anymore

Perhaps "Mama Tried" could be taken as a gloss on the parable of the prodigal son. But in that biblical story, the rebel returns home in the end and finds forgiveness. Haggard's incarcerated narrator never returns, not even in spirit. He's as resigned in the last line as he was in the first. "She tried to raise me right," the last verse reiterates, "but I refused." The implication is that he's still refusing. Hardheaded refusal, as it turns out, is a theme in Haggard. In "The Bottle Let Me Down," another of Haggard's canonical songs, he sits and laments his chosen path, but you never once suspect he'll go searching for answers anywhere else, and certainly not in the family Bible.

Haggard is hardly the only country dissenter. In recent years, country artists have become more explicit about religious ambivalence, even antipathy. "There's church bells ringin' down the road and we ain't goin'," Miranda Lambert casually boasts in "Another Sunday in the South." In "My Church," Maren Morris takes the sacrilege a step further. "I've cussed on a Sunday," she begins,

> I've cheated and I've lied
> I've fallen down from grace
> A few too many times

Then there's Sturgill Simpson, who, as if amplifying the defiance of "Mama Tried"–era Haggard, proclaims, on his alt-country album *Metamodern Sounds in Country Music*:

> I keep drinking myself silly
> Only way for this hillbilly
> And I thank God for this here life of sin

To be sure, there has always been an evangelistic strain in country music. It's there in Carrie Underwood's baptism anthem "Something in the Water"; there, more disarmingly, in Thomas Rhett's "Beer with Jesus," in which a young seeker relays the questions he'd like to ask the Messiah over cold ones, among them, "How'd you turn the other cheek?" and "What happens when life ends?" And yet, insofar as country music takes cues from the hymnal, it has tended from earliest days to stray from it, to grate against it, to rephrase the edifying certainties of sacred songs into psalms to doubt and recalcitrance.

Beneath the language of love and leisure, race and hypocrisy, Paisley's dispassionate music has a vatic core. What use do we have, he asks again and again, for those old and bracing ideas of sin and repentance, mercy and salvation, heaven and hell, passion, disgust, and desperation, when we're padded—or at least happily distracted—from the harsher realities, when we're separated by generations from the financial struggles and the hard-won joys that were once the wheelhouse of country music?

On the final track of *Moonshine in the Trunk*, Paisley covers "Me and Jesus," a rousing Tom T. Hall song from 1972. Hall's original is a big performance. There's a choir, a full backing band. The rendering, however rollicking, feels utterly at odds with the lyrics, which, at root, make for a kind of smarting prayer. Paisley, who has expressed his admiration for Hall's songwriting in interviews, strips things bare. It's just him and an acoustic guitar.

In the song, a drunk man experiences a religious awakening not unlike the one undergone by the hay baler in the Flannery O'Connor short story "Parker's Back." Having crashed his tractor into a tree, Parker, previously a skeptic, runs off to a tattoo parlor and, against the protests of his baffled tattooist, gets the face of Christ, or, more specifically, the "haloed head of a flat stern Byzantine Christ with all-demanding eyes," inked across his back. Afterward, Parker runs home and removes his shirt, eager to show off the design to his wife, a self-professed religious zealot, who, at the site of the image, accuses him of idolatry and then proceeds to beat him with a broom "across the face of the tattooed Christ."

Hall's man, no more studied in the ways of organized religion than O'Connor's, walks out into the woods and "makes an altar" out of an old tree stump. It's a song about throwing off airs, about finding something of your own on the other side of losing the nothing you thought was everything, the cares and concerns of other people be damned. "Me and Jesus," Paisley sings, without a lick of irony, "got our own thing going / And we don't need anybody to tell us what it's all about."

THE ONES ABOUT FLOWERS

My buddy Nick swears that "Chiseled in Stone" by Vern Gosdin is the saddest country song ever written. "You ran cryin' to the bedroom," it begins:

> I ran off to the bar
> Another piece of heaven gone to hell
> The words we spoke in anger
> Just tore my world apart
> And I sat there feeling sorry for myself

It's a hell of a start. Rarely has romantic strife been expressed so concisely. What words did they speak in anger? None, we suspect, that people haven't always said. The point, I think, is that these two lovers never dreamed they'd be the ones saying them. Nobody sets out to be miserable in love.

After a modest run as a singer and guitar player in California folk-country bands, Gosdin retired in the early seventies only to rally as a solo act later in the decade. Beginning in his midforties, he sent one song after another—"I'm Still Crazy," "Is It Raining at Your House?," "This Ain't My First Rodeo"—into the top 10. "Chiseled in Stone," which won the '89 CMA award for Song of the Year, helped him mount one of the greatest comebacks in country music.

Gosdin looked like a Burt. He had Bacharach eyes, Reynolds sideburns and mustache, Lancaster air. His pliant, world-worn voice took cues from George Jones, whose vocal performances of sentimental lyrics dredged out of wretchedness a pitiful joy.

"Chiseled in Stone" harkens back to Jones's signature hit, "He Stopped Loving Her Today." In that song, Jones tells the story of a man who makes good on his promise to love the woman who broke his heart until the day he dies. Apart from Jones's singular voice, which is its own steel guitar, what sets "He Stopped Loving Her" apart is the song's narrative conceit. The story is recounted by one of the man's friends. "You know," he says in the final verse, as if pulling the listener aside and sharing a piece of privileged information, "she came to see him one last time,"

> and we all wondered if she would
> And it kept runnin' through my mind,
> "This time he's over her for good"

The device enfolds the listener in the drama. The move turns the song into a simulacrum of country music. What country does best, "He Stopped Loving Her" suggests, is what this song is doing right now, converting a private and particular sadness into a shared and singable experience, one that provides no succor but the sad music of itself.

"Chiseled in Stone," despite its grief-stricken tone, has something far more redemptive in mind. The contrition at the end of the first verse—"I sat there feeling sorry for myself"—injects a measure of expectancy, even hope, into the heartache invoked by the opening lines. The narrator was boiling when he fled the house, but now he's cooled off. What, we wonder, has changed his mind? The second verse picks up the story. "Then," Gosdin sings,

> an old man sat down beside me
> And looked me in the eye,
> He said, "Son, I know what you're goin' through"

There's been an intervention. A widower has heard the narrator venting to the barkeep and has inserted himself into the convo. His empathic overtures, gentle at first blush, amount to a jab before a left hook. "You don't know about sadness / 'Til you've faced life half alone," the old man continues, before delivering the line that gives the song its title: "You don't know about lonely / 'Til it's chiseled in stone."

In response to the old man's riff, the narrator has beaten a path back to his house, which, as it turns out, is where we've been all along, listening as he relays the fortuitous encounter to his partner. En route, he has picked up a peace offering. "So," he tells his lover, "I brought these pretty flowers / Hoping you would understand / Sometimes a man is such a fool,"

Those golden words of wisdom
From the heart of that old man
Showed me I ain't nothin' without you

I don't know about saddest country song ever, but I think "Flowers" by Billy Yates could give "Chiseled in Stone" a run for saddest song featuring a bouquet. The two numbers, at least to my ear, are in conversation. It's as if Yates, who performed "Chiseled in Stone" at Gosdin's '09 Grand Ole Opry tribute concert, suspected Gosdin's ballad had anguish to spare. "Flowers" never bagged any industry awards. It was released in '97, just as the neotraditionalist movement, ushered in by artists such as Gosdin and carried forward by Alan Jackson and Patty Loveless, was ceding territory to the pop sensibilities of Tim McGraw and Shania Twain.

"Flowers" peaked at no. 36 on the Billboard country chart and then faded from country radio altogether. Yates, who worked as a barber on Music Row before landing his first record deal, found greater success as a songwriter. Among others, he cowrote "Choices," the stunning recantation of honky-tonk living for which George Jones won his final Grammy, in '99.

Like "Choices" and "Chiseled in Stone," "Flowers" is relayed from the perspective of a brokenhearted man. But Yates withholds the details of what his character has done, beginning instead with a litany of what he hasn't. "I should've took you dancin'," the song opens, "A little candlelight romancin', with roses." Offset by that comma, by a heavy pause in Yates's delivery, the roses are key. They hang over the rest of the song, even though they don't appear again until the final line.

In the following verses, the reasons for the narrator's romantic negligence come into view. "But I was high upon a barstool," the song goes on, "I was such a blind fool, now I know it." He was up high back then, but he's humbler now. The changes are manifold. We learn the narrator has kicked the bottle and secured a steady job. He's bought "a brand new suit" to wear to church on Sundays. To hear him tell it, he's a brand new man. Our suspense grows—we wonder whether a partner walking out would in fact bring about a change of such magnitude; we wonder whether he's stretching the truth.

Where the song goes next, you just don't see coming. "I went by the junkyard," the narrator tells us. His car is there, and yet the sight of the wreckage doesn't bring back memories of a crash but rather of the scene that preceded it. "I still see you on your knees," he says,

> Beggin' me not to drive
> But I took away the keys
> And made you climb inside

What starts as a hackneyed meditation on heartache, one that seems like yet another rearranging of the tropes used in a thousand country songs, has been transfigured into a solitary graveside service. "Oh, I'd take your place," the narrator concludes,

> in this field of stone
> If I only had the power
> Look what it took
> For me to finally bring you flowers

There's a touch of gallows humor to that phrase, "Look what it took," as if the man's failure to buy flowers while his partner was living had been a running joke between them, as if all the other changes wrought by her death pale in comparison to this one gesture, which is heartfelt and carefully calibrated, if, in the end, fruitless. Flowers, after all, don't mean a thing to the dead.

The differing trajectories of "Chiseled in Stone" and "Flowers"—one regarded as a classic, the other hardly regarded at all—could be used to make the case, common among enthusiasts of traditional country music, that somewhere in the nineties the genre lost its way. Country music, the line goes, stopped sounding sad and lonesome. It lost touch with its broken heart, started looking and sounding like the suburbs. Red wine replaced cheap whiskey. The nightclub drove out the corner bar. Sadness stopped selling records, and so went all the songs about flowers.

This, in part, is the idea advanced in "Murder on Music Row," a song penned by the writer Larry Cordle that turns these perceived changes in the music into the scene of a crime befitting a Henning Mankell mystery. "Nobody saw him running from 16th Avenue," it begins, "they never found the fingerprint of the weapon that was used." The old legends, the song goes on, wouldn't stand a chance in contemporary Nashville. Nobody wants to listen to lonesome music anymore. "The almighty dollar and the lust for worldwide fame / Slowly killed tradition," Cordle writes, "and for that someone should hang."

"Murder on Music Row" was recorded as a duet by George Strait and Alan Jackson, two of country music's leading male vocalists. In 2000, the song fetched the CMA award for Song of the Year, a phenomenon that suggested the charges it leveled against the country music industry were resonant and might even signal a willingness on the part of writers, musicians, and music executives to resurrect the kind of sad songs whose death it lamented.

But who, to answer Cordle's question, should be punished for the crime? Did he have Garth Brooks in mind? Surely no artist in the nineties had done more to upend tradition, recording songs about gay rights, embracing KISS-style onstage theatricality, covering Billy Joel, enlisting Black choirs to sing backup, and even recording a pop album under the pseudonym Chris Gaines. If worldwide fame was a prerequisite for identifying the guilty party, surely no country artist was more globally renowned or more global-minded than Brooks.

In the early nineties, Cordle had written several songs for Brooks, hit songs, among them "Alabama Clay" and "Against the Grain," the second a flagrant nonconformist manifesto that Brooks seemed to take as an artistic mission statement. If Cordle was leveling charges at Brooks, he was implicating himself. "Murder on Music Row," in this sense, looks an awful lot like those roses in the hands of Yates's sobered-up "Flowers" narrator. Musically, the song insists on its traditionalism. Cue the twin fiddles and steel guitars. Jackson and Strait, for their part, swap their lines with an exaggerated twang that calls to mind Nashville vocalists of yore.

In spirit, though, "Murder on Music Row" has less in common with "Chiseled in Stone" or "Flowers" than with Jason Aldean's "Crazy Town," a hard-rocking country song that flaunts the very sound Cordle chides but which, with far more nuance and vulnerability, explores the vicissitudes of the music industry.

Sure, the industry is a murderer. "You pay your dues and you play for free," Aldean sings,

> And you pray for a honky tonk destiny
> You cut your teeth in the smokey bars
> And live off the tips from a pickle jar

Aldean presents this litany of frustration as a series of battle scars. For Aldean, even having the chance to get hammered on the anvil is a privilege that may yet pay off. "One year," Aldean sings, with a kind of wonder, "they repossess your truck / And the next you make a couple million bucks." In the end, it's the inscrutable mystery of making it in Nashville that makes pandering to the industry's demands, however demeaning they may be, necessary and maybe even ultimately worthwhile. "We love it," Aldean sings, as if speaking for a whole generation of starving artists. "We hate it. We all came here to make it, / In this crazy town."

Set against "Crazy Town," "Murder on Music Row" sounds like a griping session, the fiddle a wagging finger, the pedal steel a thrown-in towel. It wants to be the kind of sad country song it laments but is hampered by a troubling lack of historical awareness. Many of the claims it makes about contemporary country music were made, in previous generations, about, and sometimes by, the very artists the song presents as exemplars.

One thinks of Waylon Jennings and his 1975 song, "Are You Sure Hank Done It This Way?," in which he upbraids the genre for its conservatism and, in the spirit of Hank Williams, declares independence from Hank's legacy. "Lord it's the same old tune," Jennings sings,

> fiddle and guitar
> Where do we take it from here?
> Rhinestone suits and new shiny cars
> It's been the same way for years

Far from calling for a new approach, "Murder on Music Row" seems intent on dividing the genre between the traditional and the contemporary and, by implication, between the true and the false. But was there ever such a thing as traditional country music to begin with? Are we really to believe that that old sad country music is dead and buried? And what does a sad song sound like anyway?

To be sure, there is some truth to Cordle's cynical characterization of the mainstreaming of country music. It's telling that in the months before and after Yates released "Flowers," Garth Brooks charted two no. 1 songs, "Long-Neck Bottle" and "Two Piña Coladas," a pair of boozy, breezy, up-tempo anthems that sound something like the foil to Yates's marvelous, if undoubtedly maudlin, tearjerker.

And yet for all their top 40 catchiness, the essential subject matter of Brooks's songs—drinking, heartbreak, self-loathing—is undeviating. Perhaps the difference between Brooks and Yates, between nineties country and what came before, is less an issue of life and death and more like a key change. Instead of remorse, Brooks's songs are fueled by a kind of giddy delusion, an approach that isn't without precedent in the annals of classic country.

In Golden Age staples such as "Dang Me" and "In the Summer," Roger Miller yowled about romantic frustration with an impromptu jauntiness that combined Jimmie Rodgers's blue yodeling with Cab Calloway's scat. Indeed, Miller makes you wonder whether there ever was such a thing as traditional country music, when country music, to hear him sing it, is so evidently a blender of musical styles.

What I mean to say is that in country music, as in every genre, sad songs take many forms. And if, on one end, there's the grandiose, nearly baroque sorrow of Gosdin or Yates and, on the other, the insouciance of Brooks or Miller, might there also be a place for the kind of entrenched sadness, situated just a hair shy of ambivalence, that finds expression in a song such as Miranda Lambert's "Dead Flowers," a twenty-first-century addition to the heartbreak canon?

Lambert's records cover the emotional spectrum. Few singers do indignation and regret with more panache. With her whipsaw range, she is, more than any living country singer, the heir of George Jones. In "Dead Flowers," however, rage and sorrow take a back seat to ennui. "I feel like the flowers in this vase," Lambert deadpans over a forlornly propulsive electric guitar,

> He just brought 'em home one day
> "Ain't they beautiful," he said
> They been here in the kitchen and the water's
>   turnin' gray
> They're sittin' in the vase but now they're dead

Sad songs take many forms, but the saddest ones are the songs about flowers.

GETTING CAUGHT

Before our fathers lost their jobs, before the kid at school collapsed on the practice field, before our grandmothers forgot our names, before the first big uprooting, the tug of bourbon, and the crises of faith, there was a shameless season along the cattail-flanked pikes of northeast Nashville, a season as tough to fathom now as it is mortifying to confess, when our biggest concern, at least on weekend nights late, was whose house to roll with toilet paper.

We were restive, sister. We were hemmed in by hills. There were no wars to fight. High-speed internet had yet to invade the South. So, under cover of catching a movie or playing pickup in the church gym, we pooled pocket money and raked the grocery clean of twelve- and twenty-four-packs. The cashier women could have tipped off the cops. There was no mistaking our intent for a collective case of irritable bowel syndrome. Still, they shooed us through the sliding doors, perhaps wagering we might repay their clemency by passing over their cul-de-sacs.

We rolled Laura, the sweetest girl you ever met, and Tyler, the most likely in our class to find a cure for cancer. We rolled whole blocks of strangers. We rolled our next-door neighbors. We rolled Laura again. And in one ballsy feat not likely to be bested this millennium, we rolled our high school basketball coach, a Brobdingnagian who, when he got to shouting, sounded like Darth Vader passing a kidney stone in an echo chamber.

For weeks afterward we awaited a summons to his office; to our astonishment he never said a word. In fact, for all the yards we hit, for all the Bradford pears, magnolias, maples, southern pines, oaks, dogwoods, dog houses, crepe myrtles, horse trailers, fencerows, and hay bales we barnstormed, for all the reams of toilet paper we put to flight beneath complicit stars, the porch lights that winked on, and the beagles that gave chase, we got caught only once. That was the semester that Ryan, ringleader if ever we had one, came down with a broken heart to make a country singer bawl. Erin, the culprit, was a year older than us. A senior, a cheerleader. She had pond-green eyes and a geranium petal of a mouth that spread clear across her face when she so much as approximated a smile. Beauty makes umbrage unworkable. It was hard to level a grudge at Erin, but out of respect for our wounded compadre we feigned disgust, genuine outrage, and when, on a wind-strafed winter night several weeks after the split, Ryan said he wanted revenge, we were ready.

Throwing toilet paper requires force and finesse, arc and accent, the power of a Hail Mary and the touch of a fadeaway jumper. It also takes speed. Within seconds of us pulling onto the grassy shoulder in front of Erin's parents' place, the trees paralleling the road at the property bottom were turning white.

The moon was up. No one who had wheels was home. What rolls the wind didn't slap across the two-lane unspooled quick-fast from our red fingers, looped over bare branches, and rappelled down the flip side in long, taut, unbroken belts. We dressed trunks. We scribbled in tissue along the front yard all manner of stall-wall worthy enjoiners. The wreckage was compact but not inconsiderable. The tree row had become a mob of resurrected mummies.

It was time to bounce. As Ryan shot last-minute video of the mess, headlights and their icy emanations macerated the outer dark. How our shadows lengthened on the lawn as we tripped to the car! Soon we were doing seventy-plus on slender unlit back roads with Erin's father on our tail.

We ought to have shaken him easy. Ours was a newer model SUV; his, an aging half-ton truck. But somewhere, who knows where, we took a bad turn. The road and the off-road grew exceedingly foreign. *ATLiens* gave way to silence in the cab. Rather than turn round and risk a face-to-face with our pursuer, Ryan killed the lights and snaked into a driveway, tree-shrouded, a little creek flowing alongside.

In skittish silence we waited for the pickup to blow by, waited for the minutes to coalesce, for time to give sanctuary. We were right there waiting when the old man pulled in behind.

Cornered, fumbling for excuses, our bowed heads silhouetted in the high beams, we readied for a lecture, a rumble, at minimum a phone call home. But Erin's father refused to dignify our shenanigans with anything resembling ire. He chatted briefly with Ryan about cleaning up the next morning. He cupped his hand against the side window to take stock of the rest of us, climbed back in the truck and rode away.

Seldom has escape felt less euphoric. Per normal we repaired to the Waffle House to refuel and color commentate, but there was a general sense, unspoken, irrefutable, that something had ended, something beyond our dumb run of toilet-papered yards. Our picked-at eggs, our fork-gored waffles, they darkened, they drowned in pools of cold syrup, every song on the jukebox a song about a broken heart. The waitress brought the checks. They might as well have been notices of infraction. The fine for pretending to be invincible: $5, $6 a pop.

In the weeks that followed, we tried to recapture the old magic, branching into sloppier brands of horseplay—doing bottle-rocket drive-bys, emptying into random yards mammoth bags of popcorn pinched from the dumpster behind the cineplex—but to no avail. It wasn't long before our weekends had disentangled and with them our fraternity, which had been close-knit since elementary school.

We drifted different ways. Some hit the bottle. Some worked on cars. One rapped at clubs downtown. One read Camus.

Inevitably, there came a day when we awoke to find our own houses had become targets, but by then it hardly mattered, we had moved on. Finally, on the receiving end of our own foolishness, we walked with our fathers out into the fog and, like Ryan on that morning after we first got busted, began the sorry business of bagging the toilet paper in the trees.

ALABAMA'S MORTAL SOUNDS

My father, who doesn't tell me much, told me once that I was conceived on the night of an Alabama concert. Dates of conception can be difficult to pinpoint, so the strange precision of this particular recollection makes me trust it. Chances are my father would remember a concert—and a country music concert, what reason would he have to make up something like that?

He hated country music. He was from Cincinnati. He was big into classic rock, but more than classic rock, he was committed to the Cincinnati Reds. How he worshipped Pete Rose, Joe Morgan, and Johnny Bench! It strikes me now that the scruffy beauty that marked the on-field play of the Big Red Machine was, in some odd way, characteristic of his favorite bands, too. He loved raunchy guitars, three-part harmony, hair. *Let It Be*–era Beatles, to be sure, but also Journey, Steely Dan, the Moody Blues. On Side A of my father's life: "Carry on my wayward son / There'll be peace when you are done." On Side B: a four-minute guitar solo by Steven Stills.

His tastes were hardly high-brow, and yet his disdain for country music did have about it a latent hipper-than-thou. Unlike my mother, who'd come of age in the hills north of Nashville, he was from the city, not the woods. Did he even own a pair of blue jeans? To him, honky-tonks and hay bales were less physical realities than a kind of diction signifying some rusty combination of the backward and the absurd. If he ever "drowned his troubles," a phrase I never heard him say, it was in work instead of the outlets endorsed in country songs: cheap whiskey, lonely women, open road.

Alabama, come to think of it, may have been the one country band he could stomach, for, aesthetically at least, the path from REO Speedwagon to Alabama was straighter than the path from Alabama to, say, Ernest Tubb. For starters, Alabama was a country band at a time when country bands tended to be stage props for solo acts, sideshows to the main event.

In Nashville, if not in London and Los Angeles, the specter of the lonely troubadour still loomed. Sure, George Jones had a band, and Loretta Lynn did too, but when you thought of George and Loretta, you didn't think about the band, the members of which tended to be loose configurations of available players. They were rarely if ever pictured on album covers. They were never named on marquees.

Country singers were roving gamblers (Kenny Rogers), runaway outlaws (Willie Nelson), wildflowers (Tanya Tucker), tipsy jokesters (Roger Miller), highway vagabonds (Hank Snow), fed-up wives (Melba Montgomery). Sure, there was the occasional duo, but they tended to be siblings or spouses, opposing forces working out their differences in tandem. Country songs were a function of individuation. But country bands eschewed the idiosyncratic in favor of something simultaneously more accessible and abstract, a dynamic that had been unfamiliar to country music before Alabama.

Throughout the late sixties and early seventies, folk-inspired songwriters such as Mickey Newbury and Kris Kristofferson had made intricate lyrics about the diamond absolutes a calling card of Nashville country. They paid deference to Bob Dylan, Kitty Wells, Fellini, Camus. They cordoned off a corner for hippies in the honky-tonk. With Alabama, however, lyrical derring-do and emotional complexity made way for mass appeal. Tone poems about rural poverty and romantic bankruptcy gave way to drum-driven, big hook anthems. Alabama was more interested in making hits than making statements, and no country band ever made more hits.

All told, Alabama sent forty singles to the top of the country charts. To date, they have sold more than seventy million records. With their roisterous fiddle solos and Queen-style drum patterns, songs such as "Tennessee River," "Dixieland

Delight," and "Mountain Music" crossed over to pop radio. They played Johnny Carson's *Tonight Show*. They got a star on the Hollywood Walk of Fame. In 1989, the Academy of Country Music named them the artist of the decade.

Among the hallmarks of Alabama's drolly adrenal brand of country rock was an overt sensuality cribbed from disco and Muscle Shoals–style R&B. There's a reason Brad Paisley called his 2011 hit about making out in cars "Old Alabama." No country act since Conway Twitty had sung so much about sex:

I got something cookin'
And I'm boilin' way down deep
While I'm hot and bothered
Why don't you give me what I need
— "Get It While It's Hot," 1977

I want to come over
I want to love you tonight
I don't care about the time
or who's wrong or who's right
— "I Wanna Come Over," 1979

Your body feels so gentle
And my passion rises high
You're loving me so easy
Your wish is my command
— "Feels So Right," 1981

The lyrics, it must be said, look a lot more lurid than they sound. Whether singing about cheating or watching baseball from the bleachers, Randy Owen, Alabama's log-stiff, lumberjack-looking front man, performed in the same husky, North Alabama brogue. His talent was to make vulnerability invulnerable, carnality as anodyne as changing oil. He really could have been singing about anything. If Owen was able to chip away at certain Nashville taboos, it may have been because nobody really noticed.

In later years, Owen would record traditional gospel albums and give homage to country troubadours of old, and yet his legacy, at least in part, has to do with jettisoning guilt, which is to say existential struggle, from heartbreak music. In this way, Alabama departed from country's Golden Age gods, for whom the tension between flesh and spirit, the stage and the confessional, was vitally generative. The boys ushered Reagan-era narcissism into the mainstream. There was a nose-candy blear to their Panglossian MO.

For every foray into pop rock, however, Alabama was careful to give a nod to the country crowd. In "If You're Gonna Play in Texas," a no. 1 song from 1983, Owen and company seek a kind of forgiveness for losing touch with their roots, only to prove themselves keen students of Cajun music and Western swing. Jeff Cook's fiddle solo, which comes sawing through the drum beat at the 3:30 mark, references the Texas Playboys and Doug Kershaw while also nodding to "Cotton-Eyed Joe."

Even at their most traditional, Alabama projected a contradictory breeziness. In "Jukebox in My Mind," a no. 1 song from 1990, Owen likens heartache to an indwelling jukebox that dispenses painful memories at inauspicious times. Lyrically, the song is an interesting inversion of the Porter Wagoner classic, "Turn the Jukebox Up Louder," in which the narrator finds balm for his heartache in a rollicking country bar. The problem is you can't really imagine "Jukebox in My Mind" coming out of a jukebox. The slick harmonies and pungent drums water down the double shot. Plugged in, glossed up, and swelled to arena size, honky-tonk music becomes inconceivable.

In a certain light, Alabama seemed versatile; in another, disingenuous. Like the Eagles and the other southern rock bands after which they fashioned themselves, the band projected machismo on album covers and merch. Their official logo, a bulgy metallic rendering of the word Alabama, was the stuff of belt buckles and pickup truck grills. The other insignia with which they were identified was the Stars and Bars, an association from which, like Tom Petty and Lynyrd Skynyrd, they later distanced themselves.

If, at root, Alabama's music was about sex and making music, their branding oozed white southern pride. Occasionally, the two came together. "And just like the South, girl," Owen sings on "See the Embers, Feel the Flame," as if providing the soundtrack to a postbellum bodice ripper, "we're gonna rise again."

I doubt my father had such lyrics in mind when he bought tickets to see Alabama on the night I was conceived. He may not have had any lyrics in mind at all. If my math is correct, the show would have taken place around my parents' first anniversary. It's possible that it was only the most convenient way of marking a year of marriage—an outing within striking distance (I think it took place at the fairgrounds downtown) that was nevertheless far enough out of their comfort zone to feel significant. Not predictable and not spontaneous either, it was the kind of date my mother, who has lived most of her life within a ten-mile radius of Nashville, would have appreciated.

Were they trying to get pregnant? Were they in their right minds? Alabama concerts, I gather, could be bacchanals. Just by breathing, it's likely that my parents, teetotalers both, would have gotten a little buzzed. At the time, they were living in a rental house on Hollywood Street, behind the Ace Hardware. She taught kindergarten. He was working at a bank during the day, taking law school classes at night. After a year of trying to make a life together, the experience of listening to music in a big sea of people might have been just what they needed. If so, they could hardly have chosen a better band than Alabama, whose music, more than empathy, more than catharsis, promised pure escape, boot-stomping circumvention with a moderated southern drawl.

By the time I became aware of country music, around the age of four or five, Alabama's once indomitable country rock had begun to give way to a new wave of singer-songwriters and rootsy traditionalists: Steve Earl, Roseanne Cash, Dwight Yoakum, Dan Seals. As much as idiosyncratic albums such as Cash's *King's Record Shop* and Yoakam's *Guitars, Cadillacs, Etc., Etc.* were a rejection of Alabama's everything-to-everybody approach, they also certified the group as a lingering force.

The truth is that Alabama's sound had settled into the filament. By and by, their arena-country schtick had become as indispensable to country music as Hank Williams's moan and Dolly Parton's wigs. Country bands from the Dixie Chicks to Florida Georgia Line owe them a debt of gratitude. But what, if anything, do I owe Alabama? It's not as if the muffled lyrics in my parents' heads somehow worked their way into my DNA. Music, so far as I know, doesn't have anything to do with the fusion of gametes. And yet fusion is made possible, in part, by feeling, and the feeling, on that night at least, was influenced, perhaps even inspired, by Alabama's high-flying country pop.

In "After Making Love We Hear Footsteps," the poet Galway Kinnell writes about his son's predilection for walking in on his parents. "Habit of memory," Kinnell writes, draws the kid back "to the ground of his making." On occasion, I have listened to Alabama with great interest, but I have just as often turned the station, having realized that interest was never what Alabama was going for.

One time, I bought a ticket to see the boys in concert but ended up bailing after a couple of songs. Alabama, as it turns out, just wasn't my band, even though, to hear my father tell it, they'd been with me from the start. Still, I'd be lying if I denied that there are not times when, say, I'm walking home in silence or driving down some empty stretch of road after work and the jukebox in my mind cues up "Mountain Music," "Tennessee River," or "Feels So Right." The mortal sounds, however indelible, are not nearly as catchy as country songs.

THE BROKEN SONG

Three weeks ago, as we were leaving our house in the western suburbs of Chicago, I slipped on a patch of ice on the front porch steps. I had spent much of the afternoon shoveling snow. It had been a foot-and-a-half deep in places. A transplant to the polar vortex from the hills of Tennessee, I had worked for hours against my will in a state of agitated disbelief. But as I stepped out the door, my annoyance had been eclipsed by a feeling of genuine accomplishment. How many pounds of snow had I heaved? A ton? Maybe two?

The yard still looked like Nome, but on the porch and driveway we might have been back in Nashville. The wood and the walk were so clear, so passable, that I no longer saw the need to wear snow boots. I opted instead for my black oxfords. What I hadn't counted on, in the half hour it took for me to shower and dress, was that the temperature would drop substantially, turning the dampness I'd left behind into a thin but formidable layer of black ice. The fall happened so quickly, so unexpectedly. One moment I was vertical, the next I was Icarus. I landed, face-up, on the sidewalk below.

It took a moment for my mind to reunite with my body. As I came to, I was cautiously relieved. Shock aside, I seemed to have escaped uninjured. My head had missed the bottom step. My jacket had somewhat padded the impact of the fall. Even better, the kids were already in the car and hadn't seen my spill. Neither had Emily. She was still in the house. Is a wipeout a wipeout if there are no witnesses?

The one thing that ached a little was my right hand, which was out to my side now, palm down in the snow. When I lifted it, I expected to find a cross-hatching of scrapes, at worst a bloody smear from where the hand had hit gravel or frozen mulch in what, in the summer, had been a flower bed. What I found instead was my key chain, the one I'd swiped, as always, from the side table in the living room on the way out the door. It was dangling, chime-like, from my palm. It looked like leg-erdemain, sleight of hand in the truest sense, only this wasn't magic, it was blunt-force trauma. I had impaled my hand on the house key.

The key was staked into the meat of my palm. The round hilt was the only part visible. Instinctively, I reached over to see if I might be able to dislodge it by myself but when I fingered the metal, an icy electrocution coursed through my wrist and arm. The key wasn't going anywhere. It was bur-ied beyond budging. A wipeout is a wipeout with or without witnesses.

In the fifteen minutes it took to get from the house to the hospital, the adrenaline that had allowed me to greet the inci-dent with a straight enough face began to wane. The pressure in my hand intensified. It was as if the teeth had pinned all the feeling in my body to the center of my palm, which felt a hundred times bigger, heavier, as if at any moment it might just pull the rest of my body inside.

Before we left the house, Emily had wrapped my arm in a red dish towel, and when we walked into the ER, the nurses at the desk, thinking I was gushing blood, sprang to action. When they unwrapped the towel and saw the key instead, their urgency gave way to amusement. In the hospital room a few minutes later, the doctor asked whether he could take a picture to show his medical students. He said in all his life he'd never seen anything like it, and for a moment I felt special, until I realized that in the hospital special isn't something you want to be. "Seen it thousands of times." "Fixed one of these just this morning." In a hospital, that's what you want to hear.

In any case, as the doctor produced his phone and the nurses gawked, I glimpsed down and for the first time since the accident saw my bloody fingers cupped around the buried key, and the image just seared itself into my brain. It was gruesome and surreal, Max Ernst meets *Pan's Labyrinth*. A key in a hand. What exactly would it be trying to unlock?

Pain, it turns out. The nerve-frying kind. I was expecting the doctor to remove it with a scalpel, something surgical, something super precise, but after administering a weak numbing agent to my right palm, he just seized on the hilt and yanked. I was in agony. I moaned and flailed. I needed a swill of whiskey. I needed a bullet to gnaw. It took five pulls, each one harder and rougher than the one before, and you should have heard the pop when the key finally gave. It exploded out of my hand. If a nurse hadn't been standing behind him, the doctor might very well have flown through the wall.

The relief was intense and immediate, but ever since, there's been a cold burn through the middle phalanx of my ring and middle fingers, and I still can't feel a thing in the tips. I take medicine twice daily with Saltines. It lowers the voltage in my hand but revs up my mind. It's like shooting a spiked double espresso before bed.

Most nights, rather than roll around and risk waking Emily, I've been slipping out to the living room to listen to old records. Apart from the muted once-an-hour rumbling of the Chicago-bound trains and the occasional patter of a spooked daughter on the stairs, the music is sequestered, and I can mull over the words.

There's a song on one of my Hank Williams records called "Everything's Okay." It's one of those numbers that Hank talk-sings in the guise of his alter ego, Luke the Drifter. The song is about a run-in with a relative whose setbacks are bested only by his resourcefulness. "The porch rotted down, that's more expense," he tells Luke,

The darned old mule he tore down the fence
The mortgage is due and I can't pay
But we're still a-livin,' so everything's okay

As the song progresses, and the verses pile on, the do-gooder's situation grows ridiculously dire. Even so, he is indomitable. From his perspective, anything short of death, however hideous, is a reprieve, which is to say a significant improvement over the alternative. Hank's tremulous voice is more heartening than his lyrics. It tells me he's struggling to hear his own song, that the preacher is the one who needs the preaching to.

The entry wound on my hand is surprisingly small, a little stigma in the lower center of my palm. Were I a better mystic, I'd be tempted to read spiritual import into the location, might fancy myself a twenty-first-century saint, Francis Assisi of Chicagoland, but when I rotate my hand from twelve to nine o'clock, the mark looks less like a miracle than a mouth flashing a hypodermic tongue, not so much "in nomine Patris" as "na-na boo-boo."

The gash was deep but narrow. Not wanting to risk infection, the doctor decided against stitches, so I cover the wound in gauzy padding and wrap the hand in an adhesive bandage once a day. For all its bulkiness, the dressing does make the injury look respectable. I could almost be a boxer, almost a burn victim. Even so, the bandage makes my right hand unworkable from pinky to pointer finger. To run the record player, to do much of anything, I have to lean hard on my left.

One of the things I love about old vinyl is the fraught silence between tracks, the popping and hissing of the needle through the scratched and dusty groove. It seems to me that this sound, a brief availing of mystery, a crackling lesson in patience, has been lost almost entirely in the age of digital streaming, which puts recorded music through a kind of forced conversion, polishing and quickening the sound until the old is made new.

Records, to my mind, possess a quality of divination, especially when the artist has long since passed. Take Ella Fitzgerald, whose *Cole Porter Songbook, Vol. 2* I picked up at a used record store in northern Virginia several years ago. Ella's not here, she's not anywhere we've ever been, but set the vinyl on the turntable and the stylus on the vinyl and voilà—she's a mic'd shade, an echo resurfacing, a very present absence that you can still sense, still believe.

A week and a half before the incident with the key, Emily went upstairs to tuck the kids into bed and found Rosie, our youngest, struggling to breathe. Her sister, Helena, said she thought Rosie had swallowed something, but she couldn't say what. We gave her water. We tried the Heimlich. When that didn't work and Rosie's wheezing intensified, we rushed her to the ER.

At first, the doctors were dismissive. They suspected she'd ingested something small, a penny perhaps, nothing to worry about, but when Emily pressed the issue they took an X-ray, and that's when they saw the quarter lodged in her esophagus. It was slanted like a half-shut submarine hatch. Before the hatch closed, they put Rosie under.

The quarter was minted in 1995, nineteen years before Rosie was born. Emily brought it home in one of those plastic urine-sample cups with the screw-on lids. I have since deposited the key inside as well. I can't help but wonder what else I will have added to the cup by this time next year. A toothpick? A wine cork? For now, the key and coin make an eerily normal duo. They're the common stuff of pockets, purses, junk drawers. You'd never thumb them as sources of pain and anxiety. You'd never know about the bodies they've been inside.

The urine cup, for its part, wants to be picked up and shaken, but to what end? The tuneless thuds, the discontinuous glissando, would you call it music? There's no discernible rhythm, no appreciable polyphony, and yet the expectation of rhythm remains.

Tonight, I've been listening to a song by Jason Isbell called "Relatively Easy." The acoustic melody pulls from folk. There is southern rock in the river gravel of Isbell's voice. For screwups, though, I'd put the song's narrator up against any of Merle Haggard's, up against any of Old Hank's.

He lives, this write-off, in a world of trouble, some of his own making, some not. He knows the burn of the handcuff. His best friend has overdosed on pills. One by one, the people around him have fallen by the wayside. His lover, she's had enough of his shenanigans. His stiff-necked brother hates both the sinner and the sin.

Isbell dishes out the sad litany in exquisite detail. "Dirty streets," he says, "smell like an ashtray." He remembers when his buddy, who "took Klonopin enough to kill a man twice his size," sported a "vandal's smile" and had "nothing but the blue sky in his eyes." He concedes it was foolhardy to shoot at the cops through the window of his loft apartment. I have, Isbell goes on, perhaps with a nod to Haggard's "Mama Tried," "everything to blame except my mind."

But then his mind makes a jump someplace unexpected. "You should know," he says,

compared
To people on a global scale
Our kind has had it relatively easy

And here with you there's always
Something to look forward to
My angry heart beats relatively easy

It's a jolt, that chorus. Where in the world, we wonder, has this sense of perspective come from? Has he been listening to BBC news reports out of Myanmar? Has he caught a few minutes of a Frontline documentary about the Taliban? Whatever the case, he knows enough to know that he is without an excuse. His window, as shattered as his self-regard and also as open, has become a point of connection. In one of the song's final verses, he wonders whether the "lucky man" he watches walking to work every morning is, in fact, so fortunate after all. For all he knows, he says, "he might not have a friend left in the world."

I think it's one of the gutsiest moves I've ever heard in a song. When you've broken your leg, the last thing you want to hear about is the double amputee. But even as Isbell sort of gestures in that direction, he's careful not to overplay his hand. He doesn't say that, compared to all the carnage and hardship around the world, his life has been a breeze, only that it's been "relatively" so. His heart, he stresses, is still angry. Later on, he says it's damned lonely, too. Acknowledging the woes of others doesn't right his wrongs, but it does seem to steel him against self-pity, even as it fires in him an impulse to give other people the benefit of the doubt.

The other day I read about this thing called the overview effect. Apparently, astronauts get it in space. The gist is that from way up there, where our planet looks like a blue bobber floating in a black pond, the conflicts and concerns that consume so much of our time and energy on earth suddenly seem petty, insignificant. People talk about the sensation as a kind of enlightenment. I guess the idea is that if we could just give everyone the chance to see the world from that remove, then all our problems, except the penultimate problem of how to ensure the continued existence of our planet, would go away. But if the man in the song made that trip, I don't think he would be as taken up with how the tanks and the fences fade from view so much as with how the wars raging in his lonely heart go right on raging, even at eight hundred thousand feet.

What Isbell says—and I'm prone to believe him—is that we don't need whiskey or a weekend, let alone a Milky Way tour, to come to terms with what we've done and who we are and what we're going through. What we need is our wits, some time, a steady heartbeat—and who can say? It all might yet break into a broken song.

BLUE DREAM

One Sunday night at a little club in Nashville, I watched an old man rise to his feet and play the first note of a bluegrass song. He had a gold front tooth. He was wearing a Savannah hat and torn blue jeans. For an hour, maybe more, he'd been fingering his guitar in the corner while mandolin, banjo, dobro, fiddle, and bass fiddle players traded solos, and the crowd, a couple hundred flush, nodded along.

From time to time, he had gazed up from his instrument, pushed back his hat, and surveyed the room. Strings of white lights crisscrossed the low ceiling tiles. The walls were papered in ragged concert bills. Onlookers sat around folding tables in folding chairs and old church pews. Neon signs, a letter burned out here, another flickering there, flashed BUD N PIZZA, Bud Light Longnecks, Stroh's Stroh's Stroh's Cold Strong Beer. Now, at a lull in the jam, as musicians filed out and others filed in, he strummed and halted as if calling the house to order. Then, into the not-quite silence he sang:

> I remember the night, little darling
> We were talking of days gone by
> When you told me you always would love me
> That for me your love would never die

And it was as if the lines had lit a fuse.

First, the inner circle of pickers and then the outer circle and then what felt like the whole room had joined in the singing, and even the ones not singing were sort of mouthing the words, and I wondered how they all knew them, the ones playing and the ones singing along, and about how long it had been since the song had first been performed here, and about how many times it had been performed since, and about how, during that span, mayors and governors and presidents had come and gone, big floods and bad tornadoes, too, and still voices had been filling this room and others like it in places such as New Orleans and Brooklyn, Lisbon and Bamako, and I thought that whatever else we could have been doing to each other or apart from each other or with each other at that very moment, we could have been doing a lot worse, and possibly not much better, than singing, if not in perfect harmony, then at least in rough unison:

> Oh they tell me your love is like a flower
> In the springtime blossoms so fair
> In the fall they wither away, dear
> And they tell me that's the way of your love

ACKNOWLEDGMENTS

This book could not have been written without the support of many editors, teachers, colleagues, and friends, including Jim McCoy, Susan Hill Newton, Carolyn Brown, Berkley Hudson, Brian Ransom, Maya Binyam, Dan Piepenbring, Sadie Stein, Mark Smirnoff, Carol Ann Fitzgerald, Eliza Borné, Maxwell George, Walker Beauchamp, Boris Dralyuk, Rob Latham, Cord Brooks, Garrett Graff, Bill O'Sullivan, Drew Lindsay, Alex Duke, Inara Verzemnieks, Bonnie Sunstein, Patricia Foster, Marilynne Robinson, Richard Preston, Bernard Cooper, Vivian Gornick, Afabwaje and Philip Kurian, Bobby and Kristin Jamieson, Matt McCullough, Isaac Adams, Lois Watson, Taylor Bruce, Robert Madison, Rachel Arndt, Larry Ypil, Tony Mylnarek, Rick and Alison Gibson, Miho Nonaka, Tim Larsen, Alan Jacobs, Russell Moore, Pam Tilson, and Blake Bratcher. My gratitude to JT Gray (1946–2021), who gave me a table in the corner and let me write while the music played. To Barbara Ray, Steve Ray, and Ben and Debbie Bratcher for giving me ears to hear and stories to tell. And a special thanks to John D'Agata for throwing open the door to the essay and saying, "Have at it."

Versions of several pieces in this collection originally appeared in the following publications:
Oxford American: "Morning Waves" and "Unlikely Lullabies."
Paris Review Daily: "It's Strange the Way the Lord Does Move,"
    "Seeing Red," "The Ones about Flowers," "To Be at Home
    Everywhere," "A Taxonomy of Country Boys," "Lonesome
    Together," "Mr. Brooks," "The Whine," and "Getting Caught."
Los Angeles Review of Books: "Visions of Cash," "Alabama's
    Mortal Sounds," and "The Last Cowboy Song."
9Marks Journal: "Hymns in a Woman's Life."

NOTES

BUB

7 *But I never picked cotton*: Roy Clark, "I Never Picked Cotton," by Bobby George and Charlie Williams, *I Never Picked Cotton*, track A1, Dot Records, 1969, LP.

10 *Daddy's hands were soft and kind*: Holly Dunn, "Daddy's Hands," *Holly Dunn*, track B1, MTM Records, 1986, LP.

10 *Grandma's hands soothed a local unwed mother*: Bill Withers, "Grandma's Hands," *Just as I Am*, track A3, Sony Music Entertainment, 1971, LP.

27 *On the road again*: Willie Nelson and Family, "On the Road Again," by Willie Nelson, *Honeysuckle Rose*, track A1, Columbia Records, 1980, LP.

27 *Oh my darling, Clementine*: Gene Autry, "Oh, My Darling Clementine," by Percy Montross, recorded 1953, *Always Your Pal, Gene Autry*, track 9, Song Music Entertainment, 1997, CD.

27 *Always late with your kisses*: Lefty Frizzell, "Always Late with Your Kisses," by Lefty Frizzell and Blackie Crawford, *Listen to Lefty*, track A3, Columbia Records, 1952, LP.

IT'S STRANGE THE WAY THE LORD DOES MOVE

54 *You didn't count the cost*: Kitty Wells, "Paying for That Back Street Affair," recorded 1953, *Kitty Wells' Country Hit Parade*, track B3, Decca Records, 1956, LP.

55 *We'll have fun, oh boy, oh boy*: Lefty Frizzell, "If You've Got the Money (I've Got the Time)," by Lefty Frizzell and Jim Beck, recorded 1950, track A1, *Listen to Lefty*, track A1, Columbia Records, 1952, LP

55 *... the biggest strike in Klondike history*: Lefty Frizzell, "Saginaw, Michigan," by Bill Anderson and Don Wayne, recorded 1963, *Saginaw, Michigan*, track A1, Columbia Records, 1964, LP.

56 *I'll be true*: Lefty Frizzell, "I Love You a Thousand Ways," by Lefty Frizzell and Jim Beck, recorded 1950, *Listen to Lefty*, track A1, Columbia Records, 1952, LP.

56 *Sister says she's hungry*: Lefty Frizzell, "There's No Food in This House," by Merle Kilgore, *Saginaw, Michigan*, track A4, Columbia Records, 1964, LP.

VISIONS OF CASH

68 *Just poor people, that's all we were*: Johnny Cash, "Daddy Sang Bass," by Carl Perkins, recorded 1968, *The Holy Land*, track B1, Columbia Records, 1969, LP.

70 *I killed a man, they said*: Johnny Cash, "Sam Hall," *American IV: The Man Comes Around*, track 9, American Recordings and Universal Records, 2002, CD.

70 *But I shot a man in Reno*: Johnny Cash, "Folsom Prison Blues," recorded 1955, *Johnny Cash with His Hot and Blue Guitar!*, track B5, Sun Records, 1957, LP.

71 *We'll meet again*: Vera Lynn, "We'll Meet Again," by Ross Parker and Hughie Charles, recorded 1939, *We'll Meet Again: The Very Best of Vera Lynn*, track 3, Decca Records, 2009, CD.

A TAXONOMY OF COUNTRY BOYS

72 ... *ain't nothing but a funny, funny riddle*: John Denver, "Thank God I'm a Country Boy," by John Martin Sommers, *Back Home Again*, track A5, RCA Records, 1974, LP.

72 ... *raised on shotguns*: Hank Williams Jr., "A Country Boy Can Survive," *The Pressure Is On*, track A1, Elektra/Curb Records, 1981, LP.

72 ... *this country girl would walk a country mile*: Loretta Lynn, "You're Lookin' at Country," recorded 1970, *You're Lookin' at Country*, track A1, Decca Records, 1971, LP.

72 ... *no ills ... no bills*: Johnny Cash, "Country Boy," *Johnny Cash with His Hot and Blue Guitar!*, track A3, Sun Records, 1957, LP.

73 *You get a house in the hills*: Glen Campbell, "Country Boy (You Got Your Feet in L.A.)," by Dennis Lambert and Brian Potter, *Rhinestone Cowboy*, track A1, 1975, Capitol Records, LP.

74 ... *a cotton picker*: Ricky Skaggs, "Country Boy," by Tony Colton, Albert Lee, and Ray Smith, *Country Boy*, track A1, Epic Records, 1984, LP.

74 ... *silver in the stars*: Don Williams, "I'm Just a Country Boy," by Fred Hellerman and Marshall Barer, *Country Boy*, track A1, ABC Dot, 1977, LP.

75 ... *about honor and things I should know*: Don Williams, "Good Ole Boys like Me," by Bob McDill, *Portrait*, track B5, MCA Records, 1979, LP.

78 *A couple times I said I do*: Ashley Monroe, "I'm Good at Leavin'," by Ashley Monroe, Jessi Alexander, and Miranda Lambert, *The Blade*, track 13, Warner Bros. Nashville, 2015, CD.

78 *You'd better move away*: Waylon Jennings, "I'm a Ramblin' Man," by Ray Pennington, *The Ramblin' Man*, track A1, RCA Victor, 1974, LP.

78 *And when I'm gone*: Hank Williams, "Ramblin' Man," recorded 1951, record two of *40 Greatest Hits*, track C6, Mercury Records, 1978, LP.

THE WHINE

80 *On one hand, I count the reasons*: Randy Travis, "On the Other Hand," by Paul Overstreet and Don Schlitz, recorded 1985, *Storms of Life*, track A1, Warner Bros. Nashville, 1986, LP.

83 *He said he'd been a cowboy*: Randy Travis, "He Walked on Water," by Allen Shamblin, *No Holdin' Back*, track A4, Warner Bros. Nashville, 1989, LP.

TO BE AT HOME EVERYWHERE

88 *Back through the years I go wanderin'*: Dolly Parton, "Coat of Many Colors," *Coat of Many Colors*, track A1, RCA Victor, 1971, LP.

89 *Sitting on the front porch*: Dolly Parton, "My Tennessee Mountain Home," recorded 1972, *My Tennessee Mountain Home*, track B1, RCA Victor, 1973, LP.

89 *I cried almost all the way*: Dolly Parton, "The Letter," recorded 1972, *My Tennessee Mountain Home*, track A1, RCA Victor, 1973, LP.

90 *With a suitcase in my hand*: Dolly Parton, "Wrong Direction Home," recorded 1972, *My Tennessee Mountain Home*, track B2, RCA Victor, 1973, LP.

90 *Remember all the fun we had; We're all together once again*: Dolly Parton, "The Better Part of Life," recorded 1972, *My Tennessee Mountain Home*, track B4, RCA Victor, 1973, LP.

90 *[Mama] says it sure is lonesome now*: Dolly Parton, "Back Home," recorded 1972, *My Tennessee Mountain Home*, track B3, RCA Victor, 1973, LP.

90 *They said that I could leave a tape*: Dolly Parton, "Down on Music Row," recorded 1972, *My Tennessee Mountain Home*, track B5, RCA Victor, 1973, LP.

UNLIKELY LULLABIES

92 *I fought with the devil*: Keith Whitley, "I'm No Stranger to the Rain," by Sonny Curtis and Ron Hellard, *Don't Close Your Eyes*, track B1, RCA Records, 1988, LP.

96 *I'll close your eyes so you can't see*: Ralph Stanley, "O Death," recorded 1999, *O Brother, Where Art Thou?*, track 14, soundtrack, Lost Highway/Mercury Records, 2000, CD.

THE LAST COWBOY SONG

101 *So don't fly too high in the sky*: Marty Robbins, "Fly Butterfly Fly," from the film *Hell on Wheels*, Crown International Pictures, 1967.

105 *... bullet go deep in my chest*: Marty Robbins, "El Paso," *Gunfighter Ballads and Trail Songs*, track B1, Columbia Records, 1959, LP.

107 *Can it be that a man can disappear*: Marty Robbins, "El Paso City," *El Paso City*, track A1, Columbia Records, 1976, LP.

MR. BROOKS

112 *Blame it all on my roots*: Garth Brooks, "Friends in Low Places," by Dewayne Blackwell and Earl Bud Lee, *No Fences*, track A5, Capitol Nashville, 1990, cassette.

114 *We call them cool*: Garth Brooks, "Standing Outside the Fire," by Jenny Yates and Garth Brooks, *In Pieces*, track 1, Liberty Records, 1993, CD.

114 *Hello, Samantha dear*: Garth Brooks, "Callin' Baton Rouge," by Dennis Linde, *In Pieces*, track 8, Liberty Records, 1993, CD.

114 *So when you see the cowboy*: Garth Brooks, "Cowboy Song," by Roy Robinson, *In Pieces*, track 10, Liberty Records, 1993, CD.

115 *Six o'clock on Friday evenin'*: Garth Brooks, "Ain't Goin' Down ('Til the Sun Comes Up)," by Garth Brooks, Kent Blazy, and Kim Williams, *In Pieces*, track 6, Liberty Records, 1993, CD.

EVERYBODY'S BREAKING SOMEBODY'S HEART

119 *No matter how satisfied her scream sounds*: Eric Church, "Devil, Devil (Prelude: Princess of Darkness)," by Eric Church, Casey Beathard, and Monty Criswell, recorded 2013, *The Outsiders*, track 10, EMI Nashville, 2014, CD.

121 *Whenever I chance to meet*: Charley Pride, "Kiss an Angel Good Morning," by Ben Peters, *Charley Pride Sings Heart Songs*, track A4, RCA Victor, 1971, LP.

LONESOME TOGETHER

124 *On a Sunday mornin' sidewalk*: Johnny Cash, "Sunday Mornin' Comin' Down," by Kris Kristofferson, *The Johnny Cash Show*, track A1, Columbia Records, 1970, LP.

125 *He's a walkin' contradiction*: Kris Kristofferson, "The Pilgrim, Chapter 33," *The Silver Tongued Devil and I*, track B4, Monument Records, 1971, LP.

125 *Woke up, fell out of bed*: The Beatles, "A Day in the Life," by John Lennon and Paul McCartney, *Sgt. Pepper's Lonely Hearts Club Band*, track B6, Parlophone Records Limited, 1967, LP.

THE BALLAD OF TAYLOR AND DREW

131 *Back where I come from*: Kenny Chesney, "Back Where I Come From," by Mac McAnally, *Greatest Hits*, track 8, BNA, 2000, CD.

132 *When you came walkin' up to me*: Tim McGraw, "Just to See You Smile," by Mark Nesler and Tony Martin, *Everywhere*, track 10, Curb Records, 1997, CD.

132 *Just a boy in a Chevy truck*: Taylor Swift, "Tim McGraw," by Taylor Swift and Liz Rose, 2006, *Taylor Swift*, track 1, 2006, Big Machine, CD.

135 *When it comes to brains*: Trisha Yearwood, "She's in Love with the Boy," by Jon Ims, recorded 1990, *Trisha Yearwood*, track A1, MCA Records, 1991, cassette.

136 *Drew looks at me*: Taylor Swift, "Teardrops on My Guitar," by Taylor Swift and Liz Rose, *Taylor Swift*, track 3, Big Machine, 2006, CD.

THE STUMP

138 *But this is country music, and we do*: Brad Paisley, "This Is Country Music," by Brad Paisley and Chris DuBois, *This Is Country Music*, track 1, Arista Nashville, 2010, CD.

139 *She's got Brazilian leather boots*: Brad Paisley, "American Saturday Night," by Brad Paisley, Kelley Lovelace, and Ashley Gorley, *American Saturday Night*, track 1, Arista Nashville, 2009, CD.

139 *I had a friend in school*: Brad Paisley, "Welcome to the Future," by Chris DuBois and Brad Paisley, *American Saturday Night*, track 3, Arista Nashville, 2009, CD.

140 *... laughing all the way to the river bank*: Brad Paisley, "River Bank," by Brad Paisley and Kelley Lovelace, *Moonshine in the Trunk*, track 2, Arista Nashville, 2014, CD.

140 *Inflatable pool full of dad's hot air*: Brad Paisley, "Water," by Brad Paisley, Chris DuBois, and Kelley Lovelace, *American Saturday Night*, track 5, Arista Nashville, 2009, CD.

141 *Studyin' about that good ol' way*: Allison Krauss, "Down to the River to Pray," recorded 1999, *O Brother, Where Art Thou?*, track 4, Lost Highway/Mercury Records, 2000, CD.

141 *Come to my rescue*: Don Gibson, "Sea of Heartbreak," by Paul Hampton and Hal David, recorded 1961, *The Best of Don Gibson*, track B5, RCA, 1965, LP.

141 *Driftin' out across the blue ocean*: Patsy Cline, "I'll Sail My Ship Alone," by Moon Mullican, Henry Bernard, Lois Mann, and Henry Thurston, recorded 1963, *A Portrait of Patsy Cline*, track A2, Decca / MCA Records, 1964, LP.

143 *Despite all my Sunday learnin'*: Merle Haggard, "Mama Tried," *Mama Tried*, track A1, Capitol Records, 1968, LP.

144 *There's church bells ringin' down the road*: Miranda Lambert, "Another Sunday in the South," by Miranda Lambert, Jessi Alexander, and Ashley Monroe, *Platinum*, track 16, RCA Nashville, 2014, CD.

144 *I've cussed on a Sunday*: Maren Morris, "My Church," by Maren Morris and Busbee, recorded 2015, *Hero*, track 3, Columbia Nashville, 2016, CD.

144 *I keep drinking myself silly*: Sturgill Simpson, "Life of Sin," recorded 2014, *Metamodern Sounds in Country Music*, track 2, High Top Mountain / Loose Music, 2015, CD.

144 *How'd you turn the other cheek?*: Thomas Rhett, "Beer with Jesus," by Thomas Rhett, Rick Huckaby, and Lance Miller, recorded 2012, *It Goes Like This*, track 12, Valory Records, 2013, CD.

145 *Me and Jesus got our own thing going*: Brad Paisley, "Me and Jesus," by Tom T. Hall, *Moonshine in the Trunk*, track 15, Arista Nashville, 2014, CD.

THE ONES ABOUT FLOWERS

146 *You ran cryin' to the bedroom*: Vern Gosdin, "Chiseled in Stone," by Vern Gosdin and Max D. Barnes, recorded 1987, *Chiseled in Stone*, track B1, Columbia Records, 1988, LP.

147 *You know she came to see him*: George Jones, "He Stopped Loving Her Today," by Bobby Braddock and Curly Putman, recorded 1980, *I Am What I Am*, track A1, Epic Records, 1989, LP.

148 *I should've took you dancin'*: Billy Yates, "Flowers," by Billy Yates and Monty Criswell, *Billy Yates*, track 11, Almo Sounds, 1997, CD.

150 *Nobody saw him running from 16th Avenue*: George Strait and Alan Jackson, "Murder on Music Row," by Larry Cordle and Larry Shell, recorded 1999, *Latest Greatest Straitest Hits*, track 2, 2000, MCA Nashville, CD.

151 *You pay your dues and you play for free*: Jason Aldean, "Crazy
Town," by Rodney Clawson and Brett Jones, *Wide Open*, track 4,
Broken Bow, 2009, CD.

152 *Lord it's the same old tune*: Waylon Jennings, "Are You Sure Hank
Done It This Way?," recorded 1974, *Dreaming My Dreams*, track A1,
RCA Victor, 1975, LP.

153 *I feel like the flowers in this vase*: Miranda Lambert, "Dead Flowers,"
Revolution, track 3, Columbia Nashville, 2009, CD.

ALABAMA'S MORTAL SOUNDS

158 *Carry on my wayward son*: Kansas, "Carry On Wayward Son,"
by Kerry Livgren, *Leftoverture*, track A1, Kirshner, 1976, LP.

160 *I got something cookin'*: Alabama, "Get It While It's Hot," by Randy
Owen, Teddy Gentry, Jeff Cook, and Richard Scott, recorded 1977,
My Home's in Alabama, track B4, RCA Nashville, 1980, LP.

160 *I want to come over*: Alabama, "I Wanna Come Over," by Richard
Berardi and Michael Berardi, recorded 1979, *My Home's in Alabama*,
track A5, RCA Nashville, 1980, LP.

160 *Your body feels so gentle*: Alabama, "Feels So Right," by Randy
Owen, recorded 1980, *Feels So Right*, track A1, RCA Nashville,
1981, LP.

162 *And just like the South, girl*: Alabama, "See the Embers, Feel the
Flame," by Don Cook, recorded 1980, *Feels So Right*, track B4, RCA
Nashville, 1981, LP.

THE BROKEN SONG

166 *The porch rotted down, that's more expense*: Hank Williams,
"Everything's Okay," recorded 1950, *Beyond the Sunset*, track B6,
MGM Records, 1968, LP.

169 *Dirty streets smell like an ashtray*: Jason Isbell, "Relatively Easy,"
Southeastern, track 12, Southeastern, 2013, CD.

BLUE DREAM

171 *I remember the night, little darling*: Lester Flatt and Earl Scruggs
"Your Love is Like a Flower," by Lester Flatt, Earl Scruggs, and
Everett Lilly, recorded 1953, *Foggy Mountain Jamboree*, track by
Columbia, 1957, LP.